T0301190

# Wild
# Treasures

# Wild Treasures

A Year of Extraordinary
Encounters with
Cornwall's Wildlife

## Hannah Stitfall

First published in Great Britain in 2024 by Gaia, an imprint of
Octopus Publishing Group Ltd
Carmelite House
50 Victoria Embankment
London EC4Y 0DZ
www.octopusbooks.co.uk

An Hachette UK Company
www.hachette.co.uk

Distributed in the US by Hachette Book Group
1290 Avenue of the Americas
4th and 5th Floors
New York, NY 10104

Distributed in Canada by Canadian Manda Group
664 Annette St.
Toronto, Ontario, Canada M6S 2C8

ISBN 978-1-85675-522-1

A CIP catalogue record for this book is available from the British Library.

Typeset in 12/16pt Garamond Premier Pro by Jouve (UK), Milton Keynes

Printed and bound in Great Britain.

1 3 5 7 9 10 8 6 4 2

Commissioning Editor: Jessica Lacey
Editor: Scarlet Furness
Copy Editor: Susanne Hillen
Designer: Rachael Shone
Illustrations by Elin Manon
Production Managers: Nic Jones and Lucy Carter

This FSC® label means that materials used
for the product have been responsibly sourced.

*For Isabelle: long may your inquisitive nose stay wet, your soft furry paws bound along the hedgerows while wagging your huge white fluffy tail as we search for adventures together. We still have many more to come, especially on the soft sand here at home in Cornwall, which I know is your favourite.*

# CONTENTS

## October

## November

## December

# AUTHOR'S NOTE

One of the things I love most about living in the UK is the changing seasons. There's an unspoken rhythm to the year and we watch in wonder at the transformation of the natural world: an old oak sheds its acorns on the forest floor in the winter, while the wildflowers begin to bloom at the start of spring. As we watch these changes unfold, we know, almost by instinct, that we follow the clock of the natural world.

The wildlife know this too. The chiffchaff and the cuckoo are the first to announce the spring season as they welcome it in with their song, and the grey seal pupping season coupled with the arrival of redwings signify the return of the autumn and winter months. The seasons bring a sense of comfort and familiarity: they connect us to the natural world and remind us that, despite the changes, the return of a season is just around the corner.

I'm spoiled by the nature on my doorstep, and I regularly go out (whatever the weather!) to marvel at the world around me and to learn more of its secrets. In this book, I share with you my favourite wildlife that can be seen throughout the year. Each month explores various species I have encountered, and the hidden treasures found in the Cornish landscape. These pages also capture the wild stories from my adventures in the great outdoors with my camera, and what I've learned about the wonderful nature we have in Britain.

This book as a love-letter to my home in Cornwall, and I hope it inspires you to explore the nature on your doorstep, whatever the season.

# January

# THE WILD WEST

It's 1 January, the dawn of a new year. A day for many of us that represents a time for change. A day where resolutions are drawn up, gym memberships are bought, diets are started, career goals are set, and the saying 'new year, new me' is bandied about more times than Matt Hancock broke his own Covid rules.

But many of us like to take the alternative approach to the new year, spending the day hideously hungover in bed, on a sofa or in a chair, or perhaps choosing simplicity and just making a camp on the floor. Whatever our choice of soft furnishing, or wherever we've chosen to while away our day of recovery, there is no doubt that the curtains are drawn, a Netflix series of at least eight episodes has been selected to see us through, and Deliveroo is at our fingertips, as we promise ourselves that 'new year, new me' will begin on 2 January.

There is nothing wrong with whichever New Year's Day you choose – in fact, I believe both to be equally important. Over the years I have had my fair share of the latter, being a party girl for many years before I became a 'proper person', but that's a different book altogether. . .

I now see January as a month of all-consuming and thrilling excitement, a time of astonishing wildlife spectacles that we can only see at this time of year, a wildlife filmmakers' dream. Frosty mornings are filled with robin rivalry along the hedgerows, the deep rasps of corvid rookeries, and young kingfishers darting above the sandy mudflats as they travel to the estuary as redwings fill the surrounding trees. Hundreds of thousands of starlings swirl as one against glistening pink skies as skeins of geese fly effortlessly above and barn owls quarter crystal-like fields at dawn and dusk.

These natural wonders and displays simply take your breath away. January is a month for wildlife encounters that can make you feel awestruck and unequivocally small in comparison to the natural world, right here on our doorsteps, so much so that they can make even the most uninterested say, 'OK yeah, that's actually pretty cool' (tried and tested).

Cornwall, where I live, is incredible for wildlife. And honestly, when the conditions are right, there is nowhere in the entire world I would rather be. The most southerly point of the UK, the county is famous for its miles upon miles of white sandy beaches backed by towering prehistoric cliffs, swathes of heath and moorland, and for having some of the last remaining temperate rainforest in Britain. It really is any nature and wildlife enthusiast's dream.

This New Year's Day I decided to skip the Netflix hangover floor party as well as the gym membership because I had heard whispers of something much more appealing. Just the week before I had had a tip-off that there was a species I had never seen before in real life frequenting an area about a 40-minute drive further down the coast from where I live. This was too good an opportunity to miss. So, after a quick check of the weather and a phone call to my friend, who was also keen to see this winter visitor, we had our cameras ready and were in the car on our way. . . to the wild west.

The far west of Cornwall is a world of its own, a mosaic of vast heath, bog, twisted windswept trees, Cornish hedgerows and quaint stone walls cutting through the landscape. The coast path is speckled with granite outcrops, ancient rocks that are part of the

Cornubian Batholith, a huge mass of granite that underlies much of Devon and Cornwall and began to form some 280 million years ago. This landscape is the embodiment of wild and it makes the area extraordinarily distinctive, with an open wildness that could have been written about by any great novelist or be used as a set for a high-budget fantasy Hollywood movie. The area where we are headed is known to be one of the largest areas of lowland heath in the UK and is home to a myriad of rare species including the Dartford warbler and the Perkins' mining bee, and is one of the last found strongholds of the coral necklace plant.

As delightful as all those species are, they don't include the one on our hit list today. And as we pull up into a tiny lay-by by the side of the equally tiny road (having used Ordnance Survey coordinates to pinpoint the exact location), I look out across a vast expansive windswept field with the North Atlantic Ocean sparkling behind, the winter sun getting low, and say, 'Is this actually it?'

One thing about searching for wildlife in Cornwall, and as I know in many parts of the UK, in fact anywhere in the world: it's the locating of the wildlife that is the most difficult part. It may or may not be an easily trackable species (more on that and on how to track wildlife later in the book), but if it isn't then most of the time you are going on information shared by others that isn't always spot on, or perhaps was from two to three days ago. But that is just the nature of dealing with wildlife. . . it's in the name. . . it is wild. This means that someone could have amazing views of an animal or bird for a few days in a row, but by the time you get to the location it will have moved on. We are very lucky in Cornwall, however, and have a great network of people and groups, such as the Cornwall Bird Watching and Preservation Society (CBWPS) and the Cornwall Wildlife Trust plus numerous Facebook groups of wildlife enthusiasts based locally who really help one another when it comes to finding wildlife treasures.

So, out of the car we get, the low sun on our faces taking the edge off the slight winter chill in the air. Thankfully, and quite uncharacteristically for the north coast of west Cornwall, there is very little wind today, it is dry, and it's the right time of day – early dusk – so all in all the perfect conditions for the species in question.

I walk down the edge of the field margin, the mud squelching between my wellies with each step, camera and tripod in hand. I keep looking out across the huge wild expanse, with gulls and crows circling overhead, their calls travelling for what seems like miles, and the far-off mews of a buzzard in the distance. To any passer-by this place would feel empty. It seems as though you are surrounded by open nothingness; to many human eyes an expansive, almost barren wasteland. But of course, as we know, this natural rough grassland and moorland is an intrinsic yet delicate ecosystem, one that is vital for thousands upon thousands of species, one that needs to be protected.

I keep my focus on some old stone walls as I continue along the margin that runs across open fields in front of me. This is where I had been told to keep a watchful eye: the species I'm after is possibly roosting in one of the walls, as most evenings it's said to have appeared from there.

This bird is not a resident in Cornwall, but it is elsewhere in the UK, primarily in the north of England and Scotland, stretching from the uplands of the north to the Outer Hebrides. We have by no means a large breeding population in the UK, however, with estimates of around 2,000 breeding pairs, a number that fluctuates year on year. These birds are ground nesters, with heath and moorland their favoured habitat, and out of all of its kind found in the UK this is the one species you are most likely to spot out hunting during the day. The individuals we get around the Cornish coast during the winter months are migrants from Iceland, Russia and Scandinavia, which venture to our UK shores to escape the harsh winters. They will usually arrive in late October and leave us again by early March.

I decide to stop and get my camera into position on the tripod set so that I can move it with ease from side to side. I'm so far away from the stone walls that I'm hoping, if it *does* fly out, it will quarter the field in front of me, and, if so, my position could mean that I'd get a shot of it looking straight down the lens, the shot of all shots. . .

But, just as I'm extending the tripod legs, I catch, out of the corner of my eye, an extraordinarily fast-moving bird that has appeared from nowhere, and is now on the opposite side of the field to me. It's incredibly small and nothing like I imagined – seemingly no larger than a pigeon! It is moving so fast and is so far away that I have to do a double take and frantically try to focus on it just to identify what it might be.

Then, as if it has read my mind, it turns its head and holds a prolonged glance to the side, taking a sweeping glide. I see that characteristic white and brown dappled face with jet-black plumage circling two piercing bright yellow eyes. It is a short-eared owl.

The excitement is palpable, and my heart is racing. The feeling of seeing a wild species for the first time is something indescribable – it's as if a wave of adrenaline, amazement and pure joy washes over you. And for that moment in time, there is nothing else in the world. I watch it twist and turn with speed across the open moors, thinking that I hadn't realized just how small they were, and I absolutely didn't think it would move this fast. I knew they were around the same size as barn owls, but when you haven't caught a glimpse of a particular species before they can be very different to what you imagine.

Sadly, though, this short-eared owl had other ideas, and after I'd been able to watch it with reasonable clarity for roughly ten minutes, it disappeared up over the brow of the moor onto another field far in the distance. In this instance, I didn't get the shot of all shots – in fact, I didn't get any shots at all – but I did see my first short-eared owl in the wild. A day I will never forget for the rest of my life.

And to think I could have drawn the curtains and watched Netflix on this New Year's Day, as I tried to piece together the previous night. Instead, I not only had an unforgettable wildlife encounter, but also a wildlife *first*. Sometimes, the sofa and Netflix can wait. The phrase 'new year, new me' should be replaced with 'new year, new wildlife adventures' – the best type of New Year's resolution.

# WINTER SURPRISES

With the sunrises throughout January greeting us politely at around 8am each morning, I'm thankful that I don't have to get up at 3am to catch the pre-dawn, one of the best times of day for wildlife. The blue hour.

It is twilight: that eerily haunting and enchanting time of day, just before the sun rises and just after the sun sets. It is aptly named the blue hour, given the colour of the sky, but the actual duration is only 20 to 30 minutes. (I guess 'the blue hour' sounds a lot better than 'the blue sometimes 20 minutes sometimes 30 minutes bit of the day'! – it just doesn't have quite the same ring to it, does it?) But catching this magical time is a lot easier during the winter months and it's a dream for wildlife photography and filmmaking.

This morning I woke up at 6am, knowing that the site I plan to get to is around a 35-minute drive from my house, north up the coast. Leaving by 6.30am should give me ample time to set up and be in position for blue hour, full dawn and any wildlife that should appear.

Walmsley bird sanctuary is one of Cornwall's hidden wildlife gems. Tucked away behind the bustling beach tourist hotspots of Rock, Padstow and Polzeath, the site is located adjacent to the Camel Estuary on the fringes of Wadebridge, and is part of Amble Marshes, a designated Site of Special Scientific Interest. It is so well hidden that even when driving along the adjacent roads a passer-by would have no clue it was there, concealed as it is by hedgerows, trees and fields, but it is a secret world brimming with wildlife. It's an expansive wetland area that also benefits from tidal currents, which make the marshes tidal themselves and so perfect for birdwatching, as the tides push many waders up to the sanctuary at certain times of the day.

Walmsley has now become one of the most vital and acclaimed sites for waders and waterfowl in the county. Thanks to the continued work from Cornwall Bird Watching Preservation Society (CBWPS), who own the site, and warden Adrian Langdon – who has managed the sanctuary for over 20 years and, I must add, is also an excellent photographer – it is now a thriving wetland full of birder delights, especially in the winter.

But, despite the site being known for many incredible waders and waterfowl, on this cold January morning I haven't come to film the birdlife. I'm after a highly elusive, mostly solitary mammal. One that over the past few weeks has been seen regularly at Walmsley, even during the day. A mammal that is notoriously difficult to see, given their vast home ranges and primarily nocturnal habits. A mammal with webbed feet, thick brown fur, highly sensitive whiskers and a long powerful tail, and which is an excellent swimmer. . .

I arrive at the site just after 7am. It is dark, with the stars twinkling overhead and a waning moon now low in the sky. I can feel the moisture in the air on my skin. It was misty on the drive over and now I can feel the mist on my hands and face. Whooper swans start calling in the field next to me as I close the car door and I hear a tawny owl in the woodlands opposite. It is that strange, hauntingly beautiful time of day when the night hasn't yet ended but a new dawn is beginning.

The sanctuary has three hides, one of them a tower hide, and, in my opinion, the best hide in Cornwall. But to get to it I must first cross two fields, in the dark, with cows. . .

Don't get me wrong, I love cows. In fact, I love all farm animals. Yet over the last few years, I have developed quite the relationship with species of the domesticated variety. This is mainly because I have spent much of my time in Cornwall jumping fences, trudging through ditches and wandering across fields, which has led to my fair share of run-ins with farm animals, many of them being of the tricky variety. So having to cross fields in the dark where I know cows are roaming is not my ideal way to start the day.

I switch on the torch on my phone as I head across the fields, following the tiny path left by other birders, and get over the first gate. The blue light is now becoming visible but it's obscured by the mist, giving the morning an unearthly feel. The air is perfectly still and you can hear nothing but the birds: robins fiercely singing in the hedgerows, accompanied by wrens and the occasional melancholy call of a blackbird. I make it past the cows unscathed and through the next gate, and after around a ten-minute walk the Tower Hide is in front of me. I make my way up the wooden stairs and fumble in my pockets for the key to the hide door, having a small panic that I've forgotten it (which has happened before!) but thankfully this time I've remembered.

The air in the hide is filled with the smell of old wood, that same nostalgic smell that suffused old churches or schools when you were a child. It's cold as my fingers touch the clasps, as I undo them carefully, one by one, to open the wooden hide windows.

I look out across the marsh as the world begins to wake up. Out on the mudflats I see pintail, teal and widgeon starting their day with a spot of preening. A northern shoveller is already on the water feeding, swaying its spatula-shaped beak from side to side as it filters out plant matter and invertebrates to eat. The two-syllable call of a nearby moorhen carries across the marsh accompanied by the stirring sound of curlew, with lapwings and barnacle geese gathered in the adjacent field. The atmosphere is alive.

I turn the torch off, place my phone on the side, and put my camera bag on the floor as I head to open the last hide window, when suddenly, out of the corner of my eye, I see a movement next to the reed beds just below, fleeting and small, but a movement nonetheless that most certainly wasn't a bird – it almost appeared to be a flick of a tail.

No, I thought, it can't be. Number one: I've been here all of three minutes and there's no way I would get this lucky so quickly. This was always a gamble at best and I was more than happy just to enjoy the flocks of overwintering birds! And number two: even though I entered the hide as silently as I could, *if* it had been there surely it would have vanished into the surrounding undergrowth or swum away having sensed my presence. With these thoughts whizzing through my head, I open the final hide window and cannot believe my eyes. I glance down to the bank below and I lock eyes with none other than an otter!

My heart lurches and I don't even take a breath. Stunned into a state of complete motionless bewilderment, I cannot believe what I'm seeing. Time stands still and we look into each other's eyes for what seems like a lifetime, although it must have been all of four seconds, before the otter darts off the bank and under the water.

I mutter words under my breath that won't be repeated here and I start to shake. It will take me at least a couple of minutes to get my camera out of my bag and set up before I can even attempt to shoot any film. And was that it? Has the otter now left, after looking me straight in the eye? Was that my one and only chance? I try to pull myself together and whip out my long lens, and I can see something thrashing around in the reed beds. It's still here.

Then I realize another error: I've forgotten my bean bag! When filming and photographing in a hide I will always use a bean bag. I do generally have a problem with shaky hands, mainly due to the sheer excitement that comes over me when I see wildlife. When out in the field I always use a tripod, but in a hide situation it's often near impossible to do that so I often use a photography bean bag, and it makes such a difference. But today of all days, the first time I have a wild otter in front of me in Cornwall, I have left the bean bag at home.

I set up regardless, trying to make as little movement as possible, as the young otter tosses and turns around in the reeds. I think it must certainly be a young one, given its behaviour over the last few weeks. Sightings had been reported here of an otter, but out in the day, which is odd for an otter, as in this part of the country, especially in the southwest, they are mostly crepuscular and/or nocturnal. But the conclusion was that perhaps this was the animal's first year out on its own and that, quite frankly, it hadn't yet worked out how to be an otter.

Otter cubs in the wild will stay with their mother for the first two years. The mother teaches all of the skills the young need to survive: how to hunt, where to hide, and even how to swim, as swimming isn't inbuilt in these semi-aquatic mustelids but is a learned skill. The mother will start these swimming lessons at a few months old, usually by simply pushing the cub into the water. This young otter had mastered the art of swimming, but being seen during the daytime is highly unusual, so perhaps it hadn't quite got the hang of that part just yet.

I sit and watch, and the otter, while it dives in and out of the water as it hunts, doesn't seem bothered by my presence, giving me the occasional glance. Its fur glistens as the sun begins to peep through, the marsh now alive with the sounds and colours of a winter wetland paradise, and the lingering smell of old wood still surrounds me in the misty air. The otter swims in and out of the water, and even comes back onto the bank for a short time. I attempt to take some shots but it's a pointless venture without my bean bag, so I just soak it all in.

As I sit there in silence, wrapped up in a blanket of sound, with winter waders and waterfowl calling, the splashing of an otter as it hunts, and birdsong from the hedgerows filling the air, I don't even feel the cold. I'm over the moon I got up early on this cold misty January morning. Even in the winter when we don't feel like it, it is always worth getting up and heading out for wildlife, because you never know. Sometimes the winter is full of surprises.

# NATURE'S FIREWORKS

Animal movements, social hierarchy and species interactions. These are all areas of animal behaviour that have fascinated us for thousands of years. Why do lions live in prides, wolves in packs, prairie dogs in coteries, bison in herds and badgers in setts, and dolphins move in pods? These are questions that biologists and animal behaviourists have long studied in order to formulate coherent reasons as to why different species move, behave and live together the way they do. And if there is one thing we do now know, nothing in the natural world is done without reason, whether that be safety in numbers, an increased chance of a successful hunt, improved odds of sharing important resources, communication, obtaining the right to breed, having a better chance of reproduction, or whatever the functionality may be. Every single behaviour, hierarchy and living arrangement has one simple rationale: to secure the growth and survival of the species. But with an estimated 8.7 million species found on planet Earth and currently only around 1.8 million being formally identified, there is still so much we don't know, and perhaps never will.

It's 2.30pm in the afternoon. This week has been quite uninspiring when it comes to getting out and filming wildlife; in fact it has been impossible. Huge coastal storms with 100 mile per hour winds have engulfed the southwest of the UK, right the way from Penzance to Bristol. Ancient oaks have toppled over into roads, roof tiles have been lifted from their forever homes, and numerous photographs of children's trampolines having been hurled into neighbour's gardens are circulating on social media – much to people's amusement.

But today, thankfully, the storm has passed, and the winter's sun is once again beaming through my office window as I look out into the street. Odd bits of rubbish are laden across the road, along with dustbin lids and broken branches. I hear a charm of goldfinch fly overhead. There is a strange stillness in the air as if nothing had ever happened and the carnage of the last week is now a distant memory. And it is the almost perfect day to try to film one of the UK's greatest winter wildlife spectacles, or, as I call them, nature's fireworks.

The location that I'm heading to is one of the best places to see this miraculous display – not only in Cornwall but in the whole UK. So much so that the previous year I had a WhatsApp message from one of the producers on the *Wild Isles* series who asked if I knew anyone locally who had scaffolding as they were rigging the woods to capture a sequence for the series. Scaffolding? In the woods? It did make me laugh. The magic of wildlife filmmaking! But it is, to my knowledge, one of the only places in the UK where this species congregates in their thousands, to roost in pine trees surrounded by undulating moorland and the second-highest point in the entirety of Cornwall. It is nothing short of spectacular (and you will be pleased to know that they got their sequence!).

Desperate to get outside into nature I close my laptop, call my friend, and pack my camera bag. From Newquay, where I live, it takes around an hour to get to the location, and, with the sun due to set just before 5pm, we decide to hit the road.

Along the winding roads up the north coast the landscape is speckled with the first bright yellow flowers of common gorse, snowdrops are in bloom, and even the occasional daffodil is attempting to show their first vibrant petals along the road verges. You would never think that just the day before this landscape was shrouded in relentless rain, with winds charging off the North Atlantic coast that even the hardiest of species would have struggled in.

As we pull up to the location, I get a rush of excitement. It's that same type of excitement you had as a child when you came down on Christmas morning and saw the tree surrounded by presents, or when you were given your first pet, and is one of the most wholesome feelings of simply pure happiness – one I wish we could bottle and give to those who don't feel that connection to the natural world.

We pull up and step out of the car. The sky on the horizon is beginning to show shades of dusty pink and orange. It couldn't be more perfect. Not only have I arrived at one of my favourite wildlife sites in Cornwall having not been able to leave the house for a week, but, to top it off, there's going to be a pink sky!

If you have followed my Instagram for a while, you will know that a pink sky is my ride or die. It is wholeheartedly, categorically, one of my favourite things in the entire world, apart from fox cubs (more on them later).

If the weather is clear during the winter months when the sun begins to set and descends towards the horizon, a magical transformation takes place in the sky – hues of pink and crimson wash over the open landscape, transforming the familiar daytime blue into a breathtaking display of colours that seem to dance with the fading light, a result of the scattering of sunlight by the Earth's atmosphere. The shorter, blue wavelengths are scattered to such an extent that the longer, red wavelengths come to dominate, painting the sky with a vivid palette that is like no other. It is the perfect dusk.

Standing along the banks by the side of the road overlooking the open fields filled with sheep grazing, and with ponies high up on the moors, my friend and I are not alone, as other cars pull up and try to get a spot. They too have heard about this magical display. Today it is particularly busy, and I don't think I've been the only one stuck indoors all week waiting for the storm to pass.

As we wait with the other watchers you can feel everyone's anticipation. This has to be, in my mind, one of those wildlife displays that really does have the ability to captivate and enthral even the most unlikely champion of the natural world, and the fact that we here in the UK are able to see it on our doorsteps is something incredibly special.

'They're coming!' shouts a small boy some way up the road from where we are, but everyone hears him and the crowd looks up. The first of the starlings arrive!

Starlings can be found throughout the UK all year round and were once one of our most common birds. I remember when I was about five years old at my grandma and grandpa's in Colchester, Essex, where I spent much of my childhood, when it seemed that hundreds would come into their garden every day. I remember sitting at the window with grandma and her pointing out their iridescent plumage and how, when you get a closer look, their feathers shimmer purple, green and blue in the sunlight. I vividly recall just sitting on the kitchen floor for hours watching them. Sadly, though, they have drastically declined in the UK. Studies have shown that starling numbers have fallen by around a staggering 66 per cent in the UK since the 1970s. This can be attributed predominantly to modern farming practices as the use of harmful chemicals on the land destroys a lot of their main food source: soil-living invertebrates. Devastatingly, they are now a red-listed species.

But each winter our UK population is bolstered by starlings from northern and eastern Europe, which migrate to the UK to escape the harsh winters of their summer breeding grounds, and when they arrive they come in their thousands, forming super flocks. During the winter these flocks in the UK are a phenomenal sight. As they gather together each evening to roost, they create jaw-dropping aerial displays known as murmurations as they move together as one creating otherworldly patterns and shapes.

As we stand there, eyes locked to the skies, the different small groups of starlings arrive. Zooming over our heads, they head straight towards the pine trees. But then the magic starts to happen. Small groups converge into one, and you hear it before you see it. That is one thing that you can't truly experience when watching footage of a starling murmuration on the TV – the actual sound of thousands upon thousands of tiny wings flapping above your head. They almost make their own gust of wind, and, for me, it is one part of this spectacle that really overpowers all of your other senses – the sound.

Right in front of us, over the tops of the pine trees, adjacent to the open moors, thousands upon thousands of starlings begin to dance. The feeling of amazement as the birds move in unison is overwhelming as they create complex and beautiful patterns against a pink sky. The birds move quickly and fluidly, seemingly with a single mind and purpose. Their enchanting dance creates a sense of peace and calmness in an otherwise chaotic world. This stuff is good for the soul!

I use a 500mm lens shooting at 4K at 120 frames per second and follow the action with my lens. And what is even more incredible is how they perform these almost choreographed moves, by simply using the rule of three.

Studies have found that an individual starling will adjust its movements based on the movements of its three closest neighbours, not the entire flock. They avoid crashing by not moving too close, following their neighbour's alignment, but staying close enough to ensure they are still part of the flock and won't face any danger. There have been many theories over the years as to why they perform these displays – perhaps to generate heat or share information – but the most likely reason is to evade avian predators such as sparrowhawks, peregrine falcons, buzzards and goshawks. The rule of three is a behavioural mechanism that helps them coordinate their movements into one huge dancing swirl of birds, making predation an incredibly difficult feat for any bird of prey nearby. That said, will we ever *really* have the answer as to why they perform these displays? Who knows. But, as animal movements and species interactions go, I think the starling murmuration has to be my favourite of all time. Who needs prides of lions or herds of bison when we have starling murmurations right on our doorstep?

As we watch on until the pink sky begins to fade, the oohs and aahs from our fellow onlookers fill the air. It's not just me who is in total awe of these magnificent birds. That's why I call them nature's fireworks: a starling murmuration brings out the same oohs and aahs we hear on New Year's Eve, but this is a natural phenomenon and there really is nothing like it in the world. It's the calm after the storm, a calm that should be on everyone's winter wildlife watching list. Nature's fireworks.

# February

# THE TINY KINGLET

When I first came to Newquay I was 18. Me and my best-and-oldest friend Jessie drove down that summer after one of the muddiest, wettest Glastonburys on record for a weekend of surfing. Neither of us had ever been to Newquay before, but we had about 200 pounds between us, and Jessie had 'accidently on purpose' picked up her dad's business credit card, which we could only use for petrol, otherwise her dad would notice. I vividly remember that drive down as Jessie's car was covered in mud, just as we were, and we stopped at Exeter services. A man behind the desk dryly asked, 'Been to Glasto, girls?' as the other drivers smirked in the queue behind us. They found the state of us so amusing that we got a round of applause on the forecourt!

Together we had our 200-pound fortune, free (or rather stolen) petrol, a two-man tent, no responsibilities, and not a care in the world, with the priority simply being to have a lovely time. The world was ours for the taking. We were only going for a few days, but little did we know that we'd both end up staying, setting up homes, making the best of friends, having businesses, getting dogs and eventually moving both of our mums here too. We fell in love with Cornwall, and it became our forever home.

At that time, I loved nature, but I was far more interested in surfing, boys and getting drunk (not necessarily in that order, and I still love all of these things), and yet, needless to say, I wasn't coming to Newquay for wildlife adventures. Well, not the type of wildlife adventures I have now.

I remember, as we drove down the A392, that we came to a roundabout and saw our first sign for Fistral beach, one of the best beaches for surfing in the whole country, so we took a right and headed straight there. As we drove up Trevemper Road I looked out to my left and saw a vast estuary. The tide was out and the pools of shallow water sparkled in the summer sunlight; the golden sandbars almost seemed tropical, and the open mudflats were filled with the rich greens of samphire, cord grasses and flower bursts of lilac sea aster. I, of course, had absolutely no idea what those plants were, but I remember thinking how pretty they were. And as we drove up the road to Fistral beach, little did I know that I would end up living next to this exact estuary, and that it would become one of my favourite places in all of Cornwall for wildlife.

The Gannel estuary runs parallel to the west of Newquay and is a haven for wildlife. It is a Site of Special Scientific Interest as well as a designated Marine Conservation Zone due to its ecological significance and its importance for biodiversity. Stretching roughly three miles from Trevemper roundabout to Crantock beach, this tidal estuary flows into the heart of the Atlantic Ocean, and is surrounded by thick hedgerow, woodland on the far side, meadows and farmland. It is a world away from the pubs and clubs that are just a stone's throw away.

On this February afternoon the mizzle had set in. Mizzle is a term used in Devon and Cornwall for those grey days where the sea fog has engulfed the land and the fine raindrops create a misty drizzle that won't lift. I personally love the mizzle and find its misty embrace quite comforting. Plus, when there is mizzle that won't shift, it generally means that there is no wind, which is excellent for wildlife. This February afternoon, however, wasn't actually meant for wildlife spotting, but was a simple dog walk with Isabelle (my white German shepherd and the love of my life). Even on our daily dog walks I always have my camera bag with me as the most amazing wildlife encounters can often be when you least expect them. And today was one of those days. So, with my wellies on and coat pulled tight, pockets full of old tennis balls, camera bag on and a very excited Isabelle we headed to the Gannel.

There is something quite mesmerizing about a winter's walk on a grey day. The sky is overcast, the ground soft underfoot, and I can hear the calls of redshank and oystercatchers out on the mudflats. The bare trees without their green leaves add to the subdued shades of the surrounding landscape. The mist hangs delicately in the air and the scent of ocean spray lingers.

We walk along the northern side and I look up to the thick undisturbed scrubby hedgerow as I throw a tennis ball. The hedgerow that runs along the Gannel is relatively untouched; given that the estuary is tidal there is no opportunity for developers to try to destroy the scrub areas by building any further than the road. And during lockdown I spotted more bird species here than I have in most of our designated nature reserves. Yellowhammers, bullfinch, reed bunting, dunnocks, long-tailed tits, blackbirds, greenfinch, lesser redpolls, blue tits, robins, great tits, goldfinch, blackcaps, chiffchaffs, mistle and song thrush just to name a few – which just goes to show the abundance of birdlife a small area can support when we leave nature alone. I wish there were more places just like this.

During the winter months, ivy berries are abundant. The dark green leaves of this hardy evergreen twist through the hawthorn and holly and are covered in deep purple berries. These are a lifeline for many species during the colder months, being both highly calorific and nutritious. I watch on as blackbirds take advantage of this winter bounty, meticulously picking off the berries to eat, as well as a wood pigeon that's joined them for a snack (although the dear wood pigeon is slightly clumsier).

As I walk along the hedgerow I take in the grey day, with Isabelle at my feet. I hear a bird call that I haven't heard before, one that is very high-pitched, resembling a 'zi-zi-zi-zeep'. It sounded close, and in fact was so high-pitched that if I wasn't walking as close to the hedge I probably wouldn't have been able to hear it clearly. It wasn't anything I had heard before, none of the usual suspects, and it was the incredible pitch of the tone that really caught my attention. I turn to Isabelle with a look that says stop and raise one finger to her. She knows that this means to stay completely still and she stops and drops to the ground in an instant, looking up at me, as if to say 'Mummy, what is it?'

We stay still for around two minutes and I edge slightly towards the undergrowth, and then there it is again, 'zi-zi-zi-zeep'. It appears to be getting closer. I frantically scan the undergrowth for movement, squinting my eyes with my arm stretched out behind me and one finger raised so that Isabelle knows not to move. And then I see a tiny flash of black and white, crowned with the most exquisite vibrant orange, but it disappears almost immediately. On a mizzle-filled grey day like today the sheer brightness of that orange plumage seemed almost like something artificial, the smallest traffic light in the world. But of course it was moving so it couldn't be, so I thought to myself, it can't be anything else, it has to be a firecrest!

Firecrests are tiny. Weighing a mere 5g (⅛oz) to 7g (¼oz), which is the same as a 20p coin, they are not only the smallest bird in the UK but, coupled with their cousin the goldcrest, they are also the smallest birds in all of Europe. They are part of the kinglet family, whose name comes from the genus *Regulus*, which translates as 'little king' in Latin. There are six different species across the world, spanning North America to Asia, but here in the UK we have only two species: the firecrest and the goldcrest. These miniature songbirds are notoriously difficult to photograph, given their size. They are constantly moving in order to support their metabolisms, and they flutter around tree branches in search of tiny prey such as spiders, small insects and moth eggs. They have a preference for coniferous forest and there is a small breeding population that resides in the south and southeast of England. But during the autumn and winter we get an influx of these tiny birds from across the North Sea, and these winter migrants can be spotted from Cornwall right the way up to Scotland. But given their size, speed and movement, they are incredibly difficult to spot, and are a bit of a bucket-list bird for any wildlife photographer.

In all my years of walking this route with Isabelle I have never laid eyes on a firecrest! I quickly drop to the ground – knees first – swinging my bag round my body and with the lens already on the camera as I whip it out of the bag. I get very muddy – but this was a firecrest, and my first! Who cares about muddy wet knees!?

Crouched down by the side of the hedge I wait and hope that it will reappear. I can still hear its song in the undergrowth. I get a few odd looks from passers-by, but this is nothing unusual. After years of searching for wildlife while covered in mud, crouching in ditches, I'm more than used to a few strange looks. Then – it reappears! – this time darting about on top of a bramble bush. I take my chance, holding my finger down on the button with the highest shutter speed the light will possibly allow in the hope that I will get at least one half-decent non-blurry image. It flits around the brambles 'zeep-zeeping' away while picking off tiny insects to eat, and then it disappears. I quickly get up and try to follow it along the hedgerow, but it's gone. I never saw it again, and, in fact, I haven't seen one since.

I sit back on the ground. I'm fully covered in mud now so I embrace it. Isabelle comes over as if she knows that the moment of having to stay silent has passed and she sits down beside me. I flick through my images, and I *have* managed to get one half-decent shot! I can't believe it! Not the shot of all shots, but an incredible encounter, and memory, all the same.

As we head back home with a muddy spring in our step, we walk along the same road that Jessie and I had first driven down all those years ago. Never in a million years, when we first arrived in Newquay, did I think that I would one day be lying in the mud on a chilly February afternoon on the very same estuary, trying to photograph a bird I now know to be a firecrest. But I wouldn't have it any other way.

# UNDER THE COVER
# OF DARKNESS

The night. As the sun sets and darkness falls, the natural world around us undergoes an otherworldly transformation. Skies become encrusted with real-life jewels that sparkle like tiny cut crystals as the moon's light emits a luminous glow. Diurnal species such as woodland birds head to roost, squirrels head to their dreys, kestrels and corvids tuck themselves away, and amid the onset of darkness an entire new world of wildlife appears.

For many years wildlife's behaviour and movements weren't able to be documented at night through stills. That was until the early 1900s, when, in Michigan, George Shiras, who is widely known as the grandfather of wildlife photography, captured some of the first wildlife images at night using a home-made camera trap. George called this 'Flashlight Trapping' and used a series of wires that would trigger a camera and a remote flash that was tied up with pieces of rope. He would take photographs at night from his canoe, mirroring a hunting technique called 'jacklighting' from a North American tribe, the Ojibwa. George's images were published in, at the time, a little-known scholarly journal called *National Geographic*, but these images went on to gain worldwide attention. Flash photography was still a relatively new invention 150 years ago, and early photographers were able to make a flash by using magnesium powder that created an explosion when triggered.

I wonder how the moose, racoons, white-tailed deer and bears that George photographed felt about explosions going off in the middle of the night!

Camera trapping as a technique for wildlife photography has come on leaps and bounds, especially in recent years, helped by the advent of digital recording and developments in photography equipment. And now anyone can pick up a decent camera trap with night vision to unlock wildlife wonders and goings-on under the cover of darkness, right in their own back gardens. But camera traps have also become a vital tool in the monitoring of many rare endangered species and the use of these small black boxes is aiding conservation projects right now all around the world.

I have used camera traps for many, many years. They are, in fact, one of the most important pieces of equipment I have. Through their use I have found fox dens and badger setts, filmed roe deer fawns and tawny and barn owls, and have then been able to track the movements of species in order to film and photograph them with my DSLR. I get asked a lot about how people can find wildlife on their local patch, and my first answer is always: get yourself a camera trap – they are worth their weight in gold!

Surrounded by the ocean and towering coastal cliffs, Cornwall, in between each rugged headland, has some of the most breathtaking valleys in the UK. It's a world of woodland, wildflowers, marshy bogs and streams, and when you walk through one of these valleys it is almost as though you are stepping into a land that time forgot. If you have ever walked parts of the South West Coast Path you will have looked down onto many of these valleys while hiking out on the cliff's edge. And it's these valleys that are one of the best places to film and photograph wildlife in Cornwall, and where I'm heading this evening.

I had wanted to get started in doing my own DSLR camera trapping for a while, and the previous Christmas I had finally decided it was time. I had gone onto eBay and bought an old Nikon D3300, but I still needed some SB28 speedlights. These are very tricky to find, but I managed to locate some and got them shipped from Japan. My mate Dave already had a motion sensor and all the cables, which he let me borrow, so I was all set!

After walking right to the bottom of one of my favourite valleys for wildlife, I shimmy under some old, barbed wire and into the edges of the undergrowth. With its tall trees, thick scrub and a stream running through the middle, this is an archetypal Cornish wildlife corridor. I find the trunk of a smallish tree that is growing adjacent to the small trail. No one walks in here and this trail is made only by the wildlife. After about ten minutes of trial and error I set up my DSLR camera trap and check that all the sensors and flashes are working. I then throw an old waterproof jacket over the camera and some sandwich bags from Aldi over the sensor and flashes (the most unprofessional professional wildlife filmmaker in the world!). But, having checked the weather for the week and with conditions looking OK, I decide to leave my rather dubious camera set-up for a few days to see if it captures anything.

A few days, however, quickly turn into more than two weeks. A three-day BBC One shoot came in on the Isles of Scilly, coupled with some filming for *Springwatch* and hosting an event at the Natural History Museum in London. To be honest, I was so busy I'd completely forgotten I'd even left my camera down there! That was until I had got back to Cornwall the evening it had started to rain, and my mate Dave rang and asked, 'Did you get any night shots down the valley?' to which I replied, 'Oh shit! It's still bloody down there!'

Draped in waterproof clothing and ridden with an awful anxiety that I might have completely ruined my camera set-up (along with Dave's sensor and cables), I sprint out of the front door and pretty much run the entire way. What would usually be a 40-minute walk takes me just 20 minutes! It's amazing what our bodies are capable of when we are filled with fear and utter panic.

I slide once more under the old, barbed wire and look down at my camera set-up, soaked in the relentless and unforgiving rain. 'Oh God,' I say to myself, 'it's time to see just how good Aldi sandwich bags are.' I pull the set-up apart, throw it in my backpack and head back out of the valley and home. The journey back was not quite as spritely as on the way there, but, to be honest, I'm absolutely knackered.

Once through the front door and still in my soaking wet clothes I immediately need to see if everything is still working – which thankfully it is! And then I start flicking through my photographs to see if, first, it had actually worked, and second, if I had captured anything.

The first 50 photos had captured nothing, or even if they had, the camera was misted up, and I nearly give up looking as I think the rest will be just the same. But then the shots, which must have been taken on a different night, seem to be clear. 'YES!' I let out, as I'm sat soaking and cold on the sofa. I see the tail of a red fox! It's perfectly sharp, but, sadly, it's just the tail, not its beautiful face. I then have a badger, out of focus, and a wood mouse, also unusable. Then there's a lovely photograph of a rabbit jumping almost straight towards the lens. 'That's a good one!' I say to myself, and I carry on flicking through, elated to have captured something. I get the same feeling looking through camera traps that I did as a child opening their birthday presents: the excitement is palpable!

But then I see the face of a species that I never in my wildest dreams thought I would ever capture, and it's looking straight down the lens! A rush of adrenaline courses through me as my jaw drops open. I sit there for a while just staring at the back of the camera as I simply cannot believe what I'm seeing: a species that was one of the UK's most common mammals, but was on the brink of extinction by the 19th and early 20th century after years of persecution by gamekeepers and fur trappers. Thankfully, it is now on the up and has started to recolonize its old range, but it's a species I certainly didn't think I would get a shot of!!

'Holy shit!' I say on the sofa. 'It's a polecat!'

Now protected under the Wildlife and Countryside Act, polecats are part of the mustelid family, being related to badgers, stoats, otters, weasels and pine martens. Since protection, it's thought that these charismatic mammals have become more widespread across the UK than they have been in the last 150 years. Their mostly solitary and nocturnal habits do make them a species that is difficult to monitor, but they can now be found thriving in Wales, much of the southwest, parts of the Midlands and Scotland, and even as far east as East Anglia.

They are roughly the same size as their domesticated cousin, the ferret, with hybridization occurring in the wild. Hybridization with escapee ferrets is one factor that is thought to have aided the polecat's recovery, but of course this has meant that, genetically speaking, true polecats might at some point become extinct. But there are ways to tell if you have spotted a hybrid or a pure breed. A pure-breed polecat will have a dark patch of fur in the middle of its face that extends down to the nose, pale cheek patches and a band around the face. They won't have a white throat patch and their paws will be dark. Ferrets, on the other hand, will have dark fur on the face that doesn't extend to the nose, a white throat patch, a less apparent contrasting facial band, and often one or both paws will be white. Yet due to hybridization, when you're out in the field these will not be steadfast ways to ID them. Really, you'd have to look at DNA.

I run upstairs to my office, still in my wet clothes, and transfer the photograph onto my laptop. I need to have a good look at the picture to work out if this is a hybrid, a polecat or a ferret. I expand the image on my desktop and, to me, it looks like a polecat! I'm unable to see the paws due to the long grass, but it does have a distinctive and contrasting facial band, no white chest bib, and the brown patch does extend down towards the nose. However, the latter isn't as strong as I'd like it to be, as the brown line is quite weak and dappled in places. Yet given that fur patterns can be highly variable it really is difficult to tell. Could it have a dash of ferret DNA in it? Quite likely. Nonetheless it's a polecat: my first that looks like it could be close to being a pure breed, and definitely my first-ever photograph of one!

Elated, I sit in my office in my wet clothes for a further 20 minutes, going through each and every shot meticulously – all 896 of them. That was the only shot of a polecat I managed to get, but I'm more than over the moon with it! Hybrid or not!

After finally having a shower and getting warm and dry I think to myself just how incredible the wildlife we see at night truly is. This was my first attempt at DSLR night-time photography, and I managed to capture a species that is, quite honestly, hardly ever seen, a bit of a bucket-list animal for many wildlife filmmakers and photographers. And I can't wait to set my camera up again in the valleys of Cornwall, to, hopefully, uncover more wonders of the night: species that we rarely see yet who live alongside us, as they roam our countryside under the cover of darkness.

# RED AND PINK DELIGHTS

The UK is known to be nation of bird lovers and we collectively spend between a staggering £200 and 300 million a year just on bird seed and products to feed our garden friends. Needless to say it's a bit more than a hobby for us, the great British public; it's a borderline obsession. But quite rightly so: our birds here in the UK are fabulous. And no, they might not be as flamboyant as the Central American male Quetzal with its brilliant green plumage and three-foot tail feathers. They may not have extravagant red headdresses like the male Amazonian royal flycatcher, or have multicoloured 15-cm (6-in) bills, fusions of yellow, reds and greens, like the keel-billed toucan. But show anyone a bird feeder filled with goldfinch, blue tits and long-tailed tits, and you can't say that they don't fall in love, just a little bit. I have got into many heated discussions over the years with my wildlife friends from overseas about how 'boring' they think our birds are in the UK, but one bird that always seems to change their minds is the one I managed to stumble across today on this early February morning.

It's 7.30am on a Saturday. Isabelle and I have decided on an early long walk across the other side of the Gannel to the woodland. March is just around the corner and the forecast has predicted fine weather all day. It's as if spring is on the cusp of greeting us and today is a promise of what is to come. Being the weekend, however, means that it won't be long before the estuary is packed with dog walkers and families trying to make the most of the mild February sun, so to beat the crowds we head out just after first light.

We head down the road to a different part of the estuary where there is a small high bridge across one of the inlets. Without the bridge the water would be too deep to cross without getting soaked, even at low tide. I checked the tides before we left as we'd been caught out before, where we'd been cut off by heading across the woodland on the other side – resulting in a very long walk around the entire estuary to get back home. But this morning the tide was out and wasn't due back in until about 3.30pm – the perfect morning for a woodland adventure!

As we head across the bridge onto the open mudflats, I look across the estuary's expanse and spot four little egrets, like bright beacons of white light shining in the distance. These large birds are part of the heron family and were at one time a rare migrant to the UK, with the first official record of them being back in 1826. But over the last 30 years or so their population numbers have grown hugely. They first appeared on UK shores, mainly in the southwest, from warmer Mediterranean climates, but now they can be seen as far north as the Outer Hebrides, particularly in the winter months when their numbers swell as our now resident population is joined by birds from continental Europe and North Africa. And there really is something quite tropical-looking about them. With their bright white plumage and long crown feathers that blow delicately in the breeze, their piercing yellow eyes and black legs with yellow feet they do look rather exotic for a February day in Cornwall.

Leaving the open mudflats we head up the bank and follow the small hedge-covered path. I hear a symphony of great tits, dunnocks, blue tits, house sparrows and chaffinches all busying themselves darting along the hedgerows. Typically, most of our familiar garden birds have their breeding season between April and July, with many species attempting two broods each year, but right now everything just seems. . . ready. It's as if over the last few weeks, despite still being February, the birdsong has gotten louder, the hedgerows are busier, and all of our familiar birds are in full swing preparing for their busiest time of the year.

Walking along the path I see the first furry paws emerging along the branches of a goat willow tree, tiny silver and white tufts that haven't fully come to fruition. But it won't be long until these catkins are brimming with bright yellow stamens filled with pollen. But now it's as if the tree branches have been lightly dusted with spots of silky white velvet that glisten in the sun as an early queen bumblebee buzzes past. Goat willow (also known as pussy willow) is one of the willow species to bear catkins early in the year, and, as in all willow species here in the UK, they are dioecious, meaning that the male and female catkins form on separate trees. Their pollination relies heavily on wind to blow the pollen from the male trees to the female trees, which also produce catkins, though the females are a lot smaller, green and spiky. But insects also play a vital role in the pollination of willow trees. Hoverflies and first-emerging butterflies such as peacocks, small tortoiseshells and commas all feed on the catkins of goat willow during early spring, as do early queen bumblebees, just like the one I saw earlier. The pollen offers these species a vital lifeline as they emerge from their winter hibernation on warm days like today and willow catkins are one the most important early spring flowers for the pollinators we have in the UK.

As we leave the path and head into the woodland, the estuary sparkling in the sun to our right, it really is the perfect day. A song thrush is singing a melodious tune, one of the most beautiful bird songs in the UK, and I stop for a moment and listen to it repeating its phrases. The song thrush will start singing during the last part of winter and continue through to around July, and this undisturbed woodland habitat is the perfect environment for them. I carry on, across a woodland floor carpeted by lesser celandines, another one of our early spring flowers that are vitally important for pollinators during late winter. Their yellow star-like flowers somehow radiate a warmth from the ground upwards making the day seem milder than it actually is. But as we are walking I hear a sound in the distance, a very soft yet low call, a short whistle in a series of notes, a sound that resembles 'peu, peu, peu'. I stop and listen again as I'm hoping it's the bird I think it is, and there it is again – the very distinctive almost mournful call of a bullfinch!

I let out a tiny gasp, turn to Isabelle and say, 'Did you hear that?! A bullfinch!!'; she stares back at me, perplexed, but knows I'm overly excited so smiles and wags her tail, probably thinking that 'bullfinch' is a new word for 'ball'. The bullfinch, in my opinion, is one of the most delightful and astonishing birds we have in the UK. Their plump posture is beguiling and their plumage simply superb: the males with their exquisite red breasts, smart black caps and blue-purple wings, and the females similar but with elegant dusty-pink breasts. During the spring and summer months their diet consists mainly of tree buds and shoots. Devastatingly, this led to them being shot, and being classed as a pest, given their love of eating the buds from orchard trees, including apples and pears. So much so that in the 16th century Henry VIII made their damage to orchards a criminal act that went through Parliament; anyone who killed a bullfinch would be awarded a penny! I always knew there were valid reasons why I hated history at school.

Bullfinches are one of the 13 species of finch that can be found in the UK and are one of our largest, but, sadly, they aren't doing so well today. The decline can be attributed to loss of complex woodland habitat and agriculture intensification, and estimates state that numbers have dropped by around 40 per cent since the 1970s. They are currently an amber-listed species here. That's why seeing one is all the more special, and to this day I can still count on one hand the number of times I have seen them in the wilds of Cornwall.

I start to walk faster towards the dense scrub where I heard the call. Another reason why it is so difficult to spot them is their preference for incredibly thick hedgerow and scrub. It's in areas like this that bullfinch like to build their nests, and during the spring and summer they are very rarely seen as they stay hidden away in thickets. In recent years bullfinch have been seen more regularly up and down the UK on garden feeders (sunflower hearts being their favourite – £200 million well spent!) but seeing them out in the wild is becoming difficult, even more so given their preferred habitat and declining numbers.

We turn a muddy corner and I look out over the high dense scrub that is the interim between the woodland and the estuary. It's an untouched and impenetrable mass of bramble, hawthorn, blackthorn and gorse, just how bullfinch like it. And then I see a flash of white rump, deep red and black dart from one side of the scrub to the other. It is a gorgeous male! He's landed just out of view, obscured by the undergrowth, but I hear him call again so I decide to sit and wait. I have been wanting to photograph bullfinch in Cornwall for as long as I can remember. I have actively searched for them and have asked people if they've had any visiting their gardens, yet over the years I haven't had any luck. Could today be the day?

As I sit and wait, I hear the male calling, still out of view. This is often the way with wildlife: you can hear it, and know exactly where it is, but of course you don't want to disturb the species in question so you wait. This can often mean waiting for a very long time, often hours. But then, as I'm sat on the ground with my camera out, just to the left of where the male is calling – I can't quite believe my eyes – a female appears too!

Overwhelmed with excitement, I hold my breath. The female sits on a branch just above the male, singing her most delicate mournful song as the February sun shines on her dusty pink plumage. I think she is the most beautiful bird I have ever seen. I quickly go to take my shot, but as I move ever so slightly, she flies off along the undergrowth and out of view, and the male follows suit behind her.

Shattered at the thought that they have both flown off, I decide to sit and wait a while longer in the hope that they come back. But a while longer turns into two and half hours on a muddy path and I have to admit defeat (plus Isabelle has certainly had enough by now).

As we start the walk back home, the estuary is full of people and dog walkers, and I'm still in awe of what I've seen. Bullfinches are one of those species that look almost like paintings, even in real life, and though today wasn't my day for wildlife photography, it doesn't make it any less special.

Over the course of the following months I did go back to that exact spot to see if I could see them again, as the dense scrubby habitat seemed like the perfect place for them to nest. Sadly, I never saw them again. But one thing's for sure, I will never forget that beautiful encounter with two of the most striking birds I have ever been lucky enough to lay eyes on – the red and pink delights.

# March

# FIELDS OF DREAMS

The arrival of March is the promise of new life; a month where almost anything seems possible as winter's chill begins to release its grasp on the landscape. I love winter, but at this time of year I feel ready for spring and excited by all the wild prospects that this magical season brings. Spring flowers start to show off their incredible palette of colours and smells; ponds across the UK become bustling underwater metropolises with clumps of frog spawn; and the first hungry newts appear after their winter slumber. The arrival of our first avian spring migrants brings a change as we look up: sand martins soar through the skies heading back to their breeding grounds, being the first *Hirundinidae* species to arrive. And the first of our warblers appear, with the songs of the chiffchaff and willow warbler filling our woodlands.

March is a month filled with important dates that also signify a time of change. On 5 March it's St Piran's Day here in Cornwall, when the patron saint of tin miners is celebrated with parties held up and down the county. The vernal equinox is 20 March, a moment when day and night are the same length, marking the start of spring equinox in the northern hemisphere and autumn equinox in the southern. There is a lot to be celebrated and to look forward to in the marvellous month of March.

This is also the time of year when one of our greatest wildlife behaviours begins. It's a spectacle that is incredibly hard to see here in Cornwall, and one that you need to be up at the crack of dawn to witness. Even then, a lot of luck comes into play. But it is the epitome of March, and one that I try to see every single year.

My alarm goes off. It's 4.45am. This is a shock to the system as it's the first early alarm in the year for wildlife spotting. But as I begin to get ready, I'm filled with eagerness and anticipation. The species I'm hoping to film today is one of my favourites, and it will be the first time I have visited the secret location in almost exactly a year. Due to the rarity of this species in Cornwall, I only go to this spot once a year: first, because I do not want to disturb the small population we have here; and second, I don't want to draw attention to the site. When dealing with wildlife, ethics are my first priority, which is why I wear full camo gear, wait for hours, hidden, and stay well back from the wildlife. But given the rarity of the species, and the fact that this is my one shot at it per year, it's something of a gamble – but exciting all the same!

In early March, dawn begins just after 6am. I pull up to the location as the first light is gently cast across open fields. There is a slight wind in the air, and as I step out of the car a wren is already singing his rowdy tune at the base of the hedgerow. I sit by the side of the road for a few minutes as I set my camera up on my tripod. If the behaviour happens, I need to be ready to try to capture it as it can often happen in the blink of an eye. I begin to walk alongside the road looking into the open fields.

The first shoots of the farmer's crops are just beginning to sprout. Bright green blades of what looks to me like grass dance in the breeze, but it will be a crop of some description. These grassy blades poke their heads out of the soil on mass, as far as the eye can see. Farmland dominates the area and, looking across the open fields, you do wonder how any species can call this farmland home. And if the weather produces the right conditions, in just a few weeks' time these green blades will be at least twice the size, making it near impossible to see the species in question. So this is the perfect time of year to get the shot.

As I carry on along the road verge, I see a small obscured shape in the distance, silhouetted on the ridge of the first field. It is lighter now, but the sun still hasn't peeped over the brow of the horizon, and I can't see whether I'm looking at the species I'm after or just a large rock or clump of mud. I decide to stop and crouch down low so that just the top of my head is poking over the top of the embankment surrounding the field. I stay completely still and wait.

I'm pretty sure the object in question is moving, even if just ever so slightly, but I can't be sure. Then I see the raising of two long, large ears and a gentle slow hop, before the dark object turns into one of the most mesmerizing silhouettes in British wildlife: that of a brown hare!

It stands on its hind legs and looks for a moment before dropping back down to the ground once more to nibble on the vegetation. Yes! – I think to myself – they are here! Then I drop completely behind the embankment, my entire body including my face hugging the wet dewy grass. Now comes the question of what to do. I haven't followed the entire road around this side of the field yet, and I know from previous experience that the hares do like to congregate in the field over from this one, but for now (even though it is far away) I do not want to disturb the hare on the horizon. Face in the grass, I decide to try to move, staying crouched down and walking along the edge of the road – well, it's more of a half-squat semi-trot, while hunched over trying to hold onto my camera and tripod without face-planting the hedge. At times like these I'm pleased that many species are most active at dusk and dawn, when there are no people around, because I look absolutely ridiculous. But needs must when it comes to brown hares!

The brown hare is the largest lagomorph in the UK, and though not native they have become naturalized over time and are now an integral part of the great British countryside. Their origins are thought to be the central Asian steppes and there are varying theories as to when they first arrived to our UK shores, the most widely accepted being that they were brought over with the Romans around 2,000 years ago. But other evidence suggests that they were already present here in the Iron Age, roughly 3,000 years ago. Either way, it is known that brown hares were brought to the UK by humans, one way or another.

Being about twice the size of a rabbit they are also bigger than mountain hares, and with longer ears. They can weigh in at around 4kg (8lb 13oz) and have incredibly powerful front legs and huge hind legs that are equipped for running. The UK's fastest land mammal, they are able to reach 45 miles per hour at top speed. They have evolved this adaptation because of how they live. Unlike rabbits, they do not live in burrows underground and nor do they, like the mountain hare, change their fur colour from brown in summer to white in winter in order to stay camouflaged. They rely primarily on one thing to escape predation: their speed.

They live out in the open all year round and will make shallow depressions in the ground called forms where they hunker down to sleep as they drop their ears. I say they aren't as camouflaged as the mountain hare, but when a brown hare is lying still in a form in a brown muddy field they are almost impossible to see! It is only when they move that you might be able to distinguish them. That is, of course, unless it's March, when they put on quite the display – this is where the term 'mad March hare' comes from. It is boxing season.

I make it around the corner and am now able to view the next field across. The sun is just peeping over the ridge and the first male skylark begins to sing, soaring high up into the sky and out of view. And it's just as I thought. I slowly look up over the embankment and see not one, not two, not even three – but *six* brown hares! I had hoped the corner of the next field would be good, but I wasn't expecting six brown hares all within filming distance! So I lie down on the muddy cold ground at the edge of the field and wait.

Brown hares are famous for their boxing behaviour, which signifies the start of their breeding season, and it is a sight to behold. Two hares get up on their hind legs and jab one another, leaping straight into the air and with fur flying. It really is a powerful display. But this isn't two males fighting it out for the right to breed, which is what we may assume. Brown hare boxing fights are actually between a male and a female. If the male is too keen and is pestering the female, she turns around and starts boxing him. And let's face it, no one likes someone that is too keen. But clearly she won't box all of the males away, given that females have three to four litters each year from around the end of February through to September. The young are called leverets, and very soon after birth they are pretty much able to fend for themselves. They will stay hidden away in the long grass being fed by the mother for the first four weeks, but after that they are out on their own. This seems a pretty harsh start in life for a baby animal as adorable as a leveret, but they are a lot tougher than we think.

As I lie in wait, two of the hares leave the blades of grass and begin to move down one of the tractor tramlines. God, I think, if they were to get up on their hind legs and start boxing right now I could get the most perfect shot! Camera at the ready, not making a sound, I see them move closer towards me. But then their ears prick up. They look startled, and I hear a low deep rumble and a vibration through the ground: it's a tractor. I raise my body from my lying-down position onto my knees and look up over the field. Sure enough, coming down towards us on those exact same tramlines, is possibly the largest tractor I've ever seen in my life. The hares dart away, so fast that I can't even make out which direction they go in, as I stand up, covered in mud, my damp clothes clinging to my body.

I step away from the embankment onto the road and put my hand up to shadow my eyes from the sun. The tractor is now next to me and the farmer gives me a big smile and wave, and I, of course, smile and wave back, albeit slightly resentful at the lost camera shot. Little does this cheery farmer know that he's just ruined my chances to photograph brown hare boxing behaviour for another whole year. The hares have disappeared into the distance and the sun is up so they will now take shelter and sleep for most of the day.

I walk back down the road a little disheartened. The hares were so close and it would have been the perfect shot. But then I remember just how lucky I am to have seen any at all. They really are one of the most impressive mammals we have here in the UK, and to be lying on the cold ground just a few metres away as they slowly moved towards me is one of the most special wildlife encounters I think I've ever had. This secret spot in Cornwall is one of their strongholds, and I think to myself, well, there's always next year! I'll just have to come back again to the fields of dreams.

# LOLLIPOP NESTS

The first 'rose' of the year, *prima rosa*, has to be one of the most enchanting flowers of early spring. They can come into bloom as early as December, but it is really in March that they make their fabulous yearly debut. With their buttery yellow petals and deep green leaves, there is much folklore surrounding them; their flowers symbolizing eternal love, renewal and youth (*primus* in Latin means 'first'). In Ireland, it was thought that they helped ward off evil spirits and protect against fairies, and that planting them around the entrance to your house would bring good fortune. They were also believed to help cure ailments, wounds and headaches, and were even written about by Shakespeare.

Despite the name – primrose – these flowers are not actually roses at all but are from a completely different perennial family, their Latin name, *prima rosa*, meaning simply 'first rose'. They are nothing short of delightful, and the meadow where I'm walking on this warm March afternoon is full of them. Accompanied by a cacophony of buzzing and fluttering insects among the long tufts of grass, the meadow is alive with the sounds of spring, and yellow primrose patches dapple the ground as far as the eye can see.

Today Isabelle and I have walked to one of our favourite spots, at this time of year, close to our home. From the Newquay side of the Gannel we have crossed the small tidal footbridge and walked up Penpol Creek, through a woodland thicket that brings us out to two small meadows. This route is part of the South West Coast

Path, and if you pass the meadows you can follow through more woodland for about ten minutes and then the path leads you to Crantock dunes and beach, another one of our favourite places in the world. But today we aren't heading to the beach. What we are looking for *should* be somewhere in the dense hedgerow surrounding the meadows – hedgerow that is starting to become full of blackthorn blossom!

Each year, hedgerows up and down the UK become awash with white, snow-like flowers, tipped with thousands of bright yellow, pollen-laden stamens. These tiny delicate clusters burst out from leafless thorny branches and their sweet perfume fills the air. Blackthorn always blooms before hawthorn and will start each year in March, whereas hawthorn is around a month later, in April. And hedgerows filled with blackthorn blossom must be one of the most beautiful sights of early spring.

We sit down on the ground at the edge of the path, facing the hedgerow with the meadow behind us. The best way to try to photograph this species is to just sit and wait, and, once you get a glimpse, you follow them. This is the perfect time of year to try to photograph these beautiful little birds, as pairs will nest along hedgerows just like this and if they have built a nest, will be returning to it every 20 minutes or so. I have a hunch that some could be nesting along this stretch as I have been seeing lots of them over the past few weeks with feathers, moss and lichen in their beaks. So sitting and waiting until a pair flit past is the best option, which, on a day like today, is heavenly.

I take Isabelle's travel bowl out of my camera bag and pour her some water. As I do so I see a cluster of primroses right beside us and spot one of the most wonderful early spring insects using its incredibly long proboscis to feed. It's none other than a dark-edged bee fly!

When first glimpsed, these peculiar fluff balls can often be mistaken for some sort of bee, but they are in fact a bee mimic! They spend the winter months pupating underground and are one of the earliest bee mimics to emerge, with March and April being the best months to see them. Their appearance is an excellent example of Batesian mimicry, whereby a species that is harmless and palatable to many predators mimics the colouration, shape and behaviour of a species that can be seen as harmful and unpalatable. This clever evolutionary adaptation can be seen in many of our hoverfly species in the UK, which are also totally harmless.

When you take a closer look, however, you can see that they are remarkably different to bees. Covered in orange and black hair that gives them a furry appearance, they have only two wings, whereas bees have four. It is the wings that give this species its name, with their dark edge on the front side that looks a bit like tie-dye or as if they've been dipped in black ink. They also have a huge proboscis, about the same size as their body, which isn't retractable as it is in bees, and they use this to feed on deep spring flowers like primrose, ground ivy and bugle. I once heard someone call bee flies the narwhals of the Great British countryside – and that is a perfect description!

These insects also have a fascinating life cycle, and one that is not for the faint-hearted as it really is like something out of horror film. The bee fly uses its mimicry to avoid predation, but the female also uses its likeness to get close to mining bee nests, as mining bee grubs become the hosts for raising her young. Dark-edged bee fly larvae are parasitoids and feed on the larvae of mining bees. And to ensure that her little darlings get the best start in life, the female dark-edged bee fly will get close to a mining bee nest and, as she begins to oviposit (that is, lay her eggs), she will hover and cover them in soil and dust particles from the ground before flicking them into or as close to the nest hole as possible. Then, once the bee-fly larvae hatch, they crawl into the nest and find a host bee-grub to which they attach themselves, sucking out its bodily fluids while they grow. I mean, this life cycle is pretty outrageous for an insect that looks so fluffy and cute, but then again there is never a dull moment in nature!

As we sit and watch the dark-edged bee fly visit each of the primrose flowers before buzzing off, I hear the unmistakable call of the species that I'm here for. A very distinctive and high-pitched 'tsei, tsei, tsei, tsei' call is moving along the top of the blossom-dappled hedgerow to my right. I hear that there are two of them, one slightly further away, but the consecutive short song bursts are coming closer towards me as they dance along the hedge together. Dainty and delicate, these little balls of fluff weigh around the same as a one-pound coin and are famous for their plump roundness and a sweeping long tail that is larger than their bodies, which makes them look almost like lollipops, hence their nickname 'flying lollipops'. They are, of course, long-tailed tits.

I stay put and keep my eyes focused on the blossom. I know just how fast they are, so the best thing to do is to wait until I see one pop its little black and white head out from the undergrowth, then I can either attempt to follow them or take my shot. Much like the firecrest I wrote about earlier, long-tailed tits are constantly moving, given their size and metabolism, and are often lightning quick. During the spring and summer they are mainly insectivorous, feeding on the bounty of invertebrates that arrive with the warmer days, but during the winter they take to eating seeds, and love peanut mixes and suet at garden feeders. But, unless you have a garden feeder that long-tailed tits frequent, they can be quite tricky to photograph along the hedgerows.

I see a flitting movement along one of the branches and move my camera to focus, before realizing that it's a blue tit. I decide to take a shot anyway, though they aren't what I'm after today. And it's only when you look at, for example, blue and great tits alongside a long-tailed that you can really see the difference. Despite their names, long-tailed tits aren't members of our tit family here in the UK. They belong to the family *Aegithalidae*, which are bushtits, of which there are 13 different species around the world, ranging from North America to far across Asia. All of these bushtit species are similar in that they move around in large flocks and are very social, gregarious little birds.

'There's one!' I whisper, loudly, trying to stay quiet but not doing a very good job of it. I see the first long-tailed tit appear from the hedge with a feather in its beak. It stops, perched on top of a blossom-filled branch, then looks from side to side before darting off further along the hedgerow, and in the blink of an eye I see the second one appear from the hedge and fly right behind it. And I think to myself: they are definitely building a nest!

One of our early nesting birds in the UK, long-tailed tits will start to build their nests at the beginning of March, but they have been known to start in February. And these nests are extraordinary, intricate structures that almost resemble a bouncy dome. They can take the parents up to three weeks to construct as they fastidiously collect masses of moss and hair, which are then weaved carefully together with thousands of tiny spider webs. The outside is camouflaged with lichen and the inside lined with over a thousand feathers, making it the perfect soft and cosy nest for their chicks.

The female will lay on average between eight and twelve tiny off-white glossy eggs with brown and black speckles, and, once the chicks are ready to fledge, that bounciness really comes in handy, as the nest expands as they grow so that they almost explode out of it!

I quickly get up, grabbing Isabelle's water bowl in one hand and, with my camera in the other, begin to high-tail it along the hedgerow, following the pair as they dart in and out of sight. They are very vocal little birds, which really comes in handy; even when they are out of sight I can still hear their calls. After about a five-minute pursuit down the footpath I see both of the adults disappear into the thick scrub of the hedgerow. That must be it, I think to myself, that's where the nest is!

I sit back down at the edge of the meadow and can hear them busying themselves right in the middle of the hedge. It's an excellent place to build a nest as it's out of view and well protected by the surrounding vegetation. I know that I won't be able to actually see the nest itself, which is something I have always wanted to film, but the ones I have found are always so obscured that they've been impossible to view with my big camera. I know, however, that if I wait long enough I could get a shot of one of the adults as they appear from the undergrowth to head off to collect more nest-building material!

After around a 15-minute wait, their calls become louder again as they start to emerge from the hedgerow. At the ready, with my camera locked onto the area where the calls are coming from, I then see one of the adults dart out and perch on a bramble branch that has early blackthorn blossom around it. I tense up and focus on taking my shot, and, in what feels like a millisecond, both adults have once again darted off down the hedgerow. That would be perfect if

I actually got it, I think to myself, and frantically start reviewing my photos at the back of the camera. Lo and behold – I got it!!

As the adult was perched on a branch I managed to get the almost-perfect shot of it looking to the side. Its long tail was straight down behind it, surrounded with blossom – a picture of springtime loveliness! And I'm over the moon! Despite the amount of time I spend outdoors filming and photographing wildlife, nine times out of ten I come back with nothing at all, which is why wildlife photography is so challenging (but who doesn't love a challenge!?).

I zoom in on the image and realize that it isn't the sharpest shot, but I'm still very pleased with it as Isabelle and I head off on our walk back home. To this day, I'm yet to photograph a long-tailed tit nest properly with my big camera, but that doesn't stop me from trying every single spring. Looking for long-tailed tit nests has now become a bit of an annual ritual, and it's one of my favourite springtime challenges. And one year I know I will eventually get lucky and be able to film a lollipop nest in all of its bouncy glory!

# THE SIGNIFICANCE
# OF WEED

The animal kingdom is full of weird, wonderful and downright bizarre mating and courtship rituals. From the bowerbirds of Northern Australia with their flair for elaborate architecture, to male angler fish latching onto females with their teeth and slowly becoming absorbed into the female's body, to male giraffes drinking the female's urine before the act takes place. I mean, who said romance was dead?

But even in the UK our species have some peculiar tricks up their sleeves to attract the opposite sex. Each spring, smooth newts leave swiping right at the door, and instead the male shakes his crest while whipping his tail onto his body, wafting his pheromones around for any female to have a whiff and decide if he's the one for her. Hermaphrodite leopard slugs entwine their bodies around each other, hanging from a string of mucus, both extending blue globular-like objects from the tops of their heads – that would be a leopard slug penis to you and me – in order to exchange sperm. And we all thought Hinge was bad.

But there is one courtship ritual that happens across the UK in early spring that doesn't involve urine-tasting or strings of mucus but does involve copious amounts of weed.

It's 6.10am exactly as I step out of the car; the stars still twinkle in the sky as the approaching dawn lingers on the horizon.

This tranquil March morning I have come to a place around four miles inland from Newquay called Porth Reservoir. It's a known place for anglers, but the reservoir at the bottom quarter is set aside as a designated nature reserve with two bird hides. Porth Reservoir is a place that really feels like a secret corner of wild. Nestled in a steep valley surrounded by thick, mature woodland filled with oak, ash and alder leading down the banks to its main body of water, it is a birder's paradise. To get to it you must drive down tiny windy roads and it feels completely off the beaten track; it's just one of those places that if you know, you know.

It's cold this morning. Winter's icy grip is still not quite ready to let go, and as I pull my gloves out of my pockets I hear some black-headed gulls on the spillway gate. I can't remember one visit where I haven't seen black-headed gulls here, and at this time of year they still have their winter plumage, with just a spot of brown on either side of their white heads, unlike in summer when their heads are a full, glossy, chocolate brown. I squint and look a little closer as I can see something else move. It's a large grey heron looking eerily ghost-like – standing in the middle of the spillway. I can only recognize it by the light breeze blowing the wisps of its chest feathers.

I grab my camera bag and pull on my hat, then start to walk down towards the path that circles the reservoir as the sun makes its first appearance over the brow of the treeline. I look across the water to the other side and see a small, camouflaged tent at one of the fishing points. All around the reservoir there are mini fishing jetties with camping space behind them for the many keen anglers who will spend the night there. And over my years of coming here for wildlife I have met quite a few of them. One in particular goes into an almost full Shakespearian monologue whenever he sees me, telling me about all the wildlife he's recently seen around the reservoir, exactly where and when, even letting me know the exact branch and the exact time – to the minute! I joke about it now, but the knowledge these fishermen have of the wildlife that lives around the reservoir is second to none, and they have helped me get many shots over the years.

I walk down the path surrounded by towering old trees as the air is filled with the sound of not only woodland birds, but also coots, moorhens and gulls. There is something incredibly evocative about two different habitats meeting, coming together into one abundant environment: the sound of the woodland species mixed with the waterbirds brings an extra layer of wildness. It is total magic.

I make my way past the first bird hide, which is slightly elevated and gives a view of the area in all its early cold yet spring-like glory, and carry on down the muddy path for about ten minutes. At the water's edge to my left the bulrushes rustle slightly in the breeze and I hear a great spotted woodpecker in the woodland to my right. It is no surprise to hear a great spotted drumming in March as often they will start to drum as early as January when they begin to establish their territories. Woodpeckers are birds that are very difficult to photograph in Cornwall unless you have a bird feeder set up. We have all of the three UK species here, the great spotted, the lesser spotted and the green, with the great spotted being the most common. I have only once had the privilege of seeing a lesser spotted woodpecker, our rarest woodpecker species in the UK, over by Bodmin, but it was very fleeting. And to this day I have never seen a green. My great, great friend Chris Jones, who runs the Cornwall Beaver project, told me that he's heard the famous 'yaffel' call of a green woodpecker before out by the beaver ponds, but to this day I'm still to lay eyes on one in my home county.

The early morning sun now casts its glow across the open water. Every corner I turn, a coot or a moorhen frantically flies out from the bulrushes, making the most blasting and raucous sound that seems to reverberate around the entire reservoir. In doing so, they make sure that every single species in the area knows that there is some sort of danger around – that danger being me. I love coots and moorhens, but I do wish they could just keep the noise down. They really do me no favours when I'm trying to be as quiet as possible. If only I could let them know in advance that I pose no threat. I turn the last bend in the path and make my way right to the end of the reservoir, which is the designated nature reserve where the second wooden bird hide is built. This is where I will set up base for the next few hours.

The species I want to try to photograph today is not particularly rare – well, at least not in recent times. But during the Victorian period, due to their incredible plumage their feathers became a prized garment piece for brooches, headbands and hats, and the species nearly became lost to extinction here in the UK, with their population plummeting to a mere 32 pairs in England in the late 1800s. Thankfully, their numbers began to rise after conservation efforts and ongoing protection, and they can now be found throughout the UK along waterways, canals, lakes and old gravel pits, and at reservoirs, just like this one.

I sit down in the hide and watch as the early morning golden mist rises up from the water into the air, illuminated by the morning sun. The reed beds that dominate the end of the reservoir look almost like a painting in the golden light. A pair of mallard ducks glide just below the hide and as I look out towards the water four mute swans are joined by six Canada geese, and a cormorant stands with its wings spread, basking in the early morning sun.

Cormorants are rather peculiar waterbirds given that their feathers aren't fully waterproof, so they have to stand with their wings spread to dry them off in order to avoid them getting too cold and wet. It is thought that, as diving birds, having waterlogged feathers could give them extra weight and perhaps aid their hunting when diving for fish, but I still find that adaptation a bit odd. But, as I said earlier, everything in nature has a reason. I sit and watch the cormorant enjoying its morning sunbathe as I take my camera out of my bag, and then the species I'm after appears from the reed bed, gliding effortlessly through the golden mist, like something out of a fairy tale. It is my first great crested grebe of the morning!

Out of the five species of grebe found in the UK, the great crested is the largest, and what a stunning bird it is! With its bright white neck and face, its piercing red eyes and an ornate headdress that would put any Victorian hat to shame, it is simply exquisite. Their black crown feathers, with bright orange surrounding the face just above the neck, make them look almost as though they have a lion's mane. Who needs the Serengeti when you have Porth Reservoir and great crested grebes!

Each year at this time I come to the reservoir to try to photograph the great crested grebe courtship dance, or, aptly named, the weed ceremony. It's one of the most elaborate courtship displays in the animal kingdom: the male and the female raise their bodies upright out of the water in front of one another, frantically paddling and twisting their heads from side to side in almost perfect synchronization, holding waterweed in their beaks. In the animal kingdom this is what's known as 'nuptial gift giving', and is a behaviour seen in a wide variety of species during courtship in a bid to improve their chances of reproducing. Usually it will be seen in the male, who presents something edible or a token of some sort to the female, but in great crested grebes both the male and the female will present weed to one another. And watching it really is like something out of a fairy tale.

I lock my camera focus onto the single great crested grebe as another one emerges from the reeds. Could this be it? Will they actually do it? Over the years of coming here to film this behaviour I have only seen them do their dance once. They are very secretive and, in my experience, have only performed the display quite close to the reed bed. So I just have to sit and wait. I watch them as they swim side by side occasionally diving under to catch a fish. Great crested grebes are diving birds, but will only stay under the water for around 30 seconds at a time, and will eat mostly small fish, but also crustaceans and frogs, if they get the chance. They are supremely built for life on the water and will avoid danger by diving down to the bottom, rather than looking ungainly on land. Breeding pairs are monogamous and they will build a floating platform nest out of waterweed, which is mostly the only time you'll see them on their feet, waddling around on top of the nest in a way that is quite endearing.

I carry on watching the pair dive for their breakfasts, although I am starting to think that courtship might not be on their agenda this morning. A good 45 minutes pass and all they have done is eat. Great, I think to myself, trust me to come the one morning where all they want to do is pile in the calories. But then I look out of the corner of my eye and there is another pair much further down the reservoir, and they are shaking their heads in front of one another!

I quickly pick up my camera, run out of the hide to the water's edge, and settle in the mud by the bulrushes, the coots and moorhens doing me absolutely no favours by making a right scene as I sit down. I take some shots as the pair shake their heads – if only they were just a little bit closer! Even with my 600mm lens, they are still just that little bit too far away. And then, as quickly as they started shaking their heads, they stop. This, unfortunately, has been the trajectory of my great crested grebe mating dance story for many years now. I have never quite been able to capture it. And the pair that looked like they could have started to dance have now started to dive for food instead.

I look at my phone and it's now gone 9am so I decide to head back. And even though I didn't quite capture the weed ceremony today, it was still wonderful to be out before the sun was up. Just to see a pair start to twist their heads in front of one another is enough for me; when you see this behaviour you know that spring's great arrival is just around the corner!

# April

# ALONG THE FIELD MARGINS

It's 5pm on a warm April afternoon – probably the warmest we've had so far – and I'm headed to one of my most reliable and favourite wildlife valleys in all of Cornwall. I have spent many hours, days and weeks here watching all sorts of species. Rabbits, foxes, roe deer and badgers all live along the woodland-filled bottom and up the steep edges of the valley. And from the top of the headland, you can also see the ocean and can watch grey seals bottling in among the waves, while fulmars twist and turn effortlessly on the air. It is heavenly! However, my first trip to this exact field for wildlife was a little hairy, to say the least. . .

The previous year, when walking Isabelle along the path across from the valley at dusk, I looked up and saw, along the edge of the field margins, not one but two badgers! It was a little later in the year, around June, and I could see that the pair were moving up and down the edge of the farmer's field snuffling for snacks (as badgers do) just before the thick dense scrub and woodland. So the next night I decided to head to that exact spot and see if I could get any badger footage. The following evening I got there around 6pm and climbed over the embankment to set up along the field edge. But, knowing how flighty badgers can be and just how sensitive their sense of smell, I had to position myself more on the edge of the field rather than in the scrub, so as to stay downwind. I was also in my full camo ghillie suit with headdress, with just my eyes peeping out, camo shield on my camera and extra camo netting flung around me. When dealing with mammals, the more camo the better.

As I sat there waiting, I knew I had a good couple of hours before I'd see anything – if I saw anything at all. It was the first time I'd sat in this field and so I hadn't set up any camera traps; I had no intel on any species movements so this was a real gamble. But, knowing that badgers are steadfast creatures of habit, I thought it was worth a shot.

I sat, waiting, when all of a sudden, from around the top corner of the field came a dog barking and a man shouting, 'Oi, You! You!. . . Oi!!'

Shit! I thought. Here we go. . . My heart elevated in a split second to around 400 miles per hour and a rush of that awful fight or flight adrenaline ran through my body like I'd been electrocuted. To be fair, I was trespassing, but I had never in my life *seen* anybody in this field – ever, and it wasn't like I was there doing any harm. Still, from my experience with farmers in Cornwall, there is a fifty-fifty split in terms of how they react. Some farmers love wildlife and are more than happy for you to sit on their land or put up camera traps, and they even get excited about the photos you've taken. Others absolutely despise it, and if they have any inkling that foxes or badgers are even close to their land, they will kill them. I have some excellent relationships with some downright brilliant and fantastic farmers around the county; they are forward thinkers who know that without a healthy functioning ecosystem there will be nothing left to farm. But other farmers I know just don't even bother.

This place, however, was new to me. I hadn't bothered asking and hadn't even looked into who owned the land, so this could go one of two ways. Option 1: it could be absolutely no problem at all; or, option 2: it could be really fucking bad. I'm of the mind, however, that I know I won't be doing harm, and if fields have 'no entry' signs on them, to me that often translates as 'Welcome, please come in'. I'm not condoning trespassing, but I am a full advocate of the Right to Roam. The fact that just 8 per cent of England gives people access to nature while 92 per cent is private land is disgraceful. How are people meant to connect with nature when it's illegal to go for a walk around most of our countryside due to the sheer selfish greed of wealthy landowners, the majority of whom, in my experience, couldn't give a damn about wildlife or the environment? But that's a different book altogether, and my personal views on UK landownership weren't going to get me out of the immediate and rather daunting pickle I'd found myself in while dressed as a bloody sniper.

The very tall man and his dog started walking towards me – in fact, the dog was running. I don't know what came over me, but I knew that he probably thought I was there to cause some sort of trouble, especially given my outfit, and I knew that I needed to quash that thought immediately before his dog came and mauled me. So, in a split second, I stood up, whipping off my camo headdress and pulling the leopard-print scrunchie out of my hair. I then proceeded to wave my hair around like I was in a Timotei shampoo advert – twice – waving my hand in the air and shouting at the top of my lungs in the poshest most ridiculous accent I could muster 'Oh, hello over there! Good afternoon!'

The man and his dog both came to an abrupt halt and just stared at me in total shock. Needless to say, I don't think either of them had expected a young woman to appear from the layers of camo – let alone one wearing mascara, a touch of lip gloss and holding a leopard-print scrunchie. I can't say I have ever said 'Oh, hello over there! Good afternoon!' when meeting someone, but in that moment my fight or flight response was to become the most unthreatening version of myself and channel my inner Judi Dench.

I started to walk over and said hello to the dog, who had quickly changed from mauling mode to 'please rub my tummy' mode due to my unthreatening demeanour. The tall man just stood there looking completely bewildered. 'I'm terribly sorry,' I said, still being Judi, 'is this your field? What a lovely spot you have here.' The charm offensive continued for a good couple of minutes, and we introduced ourselves as I cuddled the dog. It turned out that I was in luck – quite possibly the most luck I could have asked for! This farmer was one of the good ones: he LOVES wildlife. As the owner of the valley, he had let it all grow up and wild purely so that animals could live there. And, after a good chat, he proceeded to show me around his land and tell me about all of the spots where he'd seen wildlife. To this day he lets me set up camera traps, and we are friends.

And this is where I'm headed today. I'm walking across the top open field as I want to set up a camera trap in order to monitor fox activity. I have two aims: first, to see if I can locate where the foxes are coming from; and second, to establish if there is any chance of me seeing cubs. One of the fields was great for fox cubs the previous year – not the field that I usually visit but still good. My farmer friend has kept me updated throughout the year and the foxes are still present on his land, so the best thing to do is set up a couple of camera traps and wait a week or so to try to monitor their activity patterns.

I turn the corner and look down the steep valley filled with thick undergrowth. I decide to get my camera out and put my ghillie suit on while I set up the traps. My experience of sitting along these field margins has taught me that you never really know what will turn up and when, so it's always best to be ready. And this evening is going to be one of those evenings. . .

My head is down in the hedge as I tie the camera to a wooden post that I had left there previously, when, all of a sudden, I have a sense that something is behind me. It's a very strange feeling, isn't it, when you know there is something or someone behind you but there is no noise. It must be a throwback to one of the subconscious senses that helped us stay alive and not get eaten by sabre-toothed tigers, or something similar. But we've all had it, that feeling that you are just being watched. . .

I stop rustling about and stay completely silent. Slowly, I start to move my head around to look behind me down the open track. Lo and behold, my senses were right! Standing about 10m (33ft) away, looking straight at me, is a marvellous roe deer buck!

We stare at each other for about 20 seconds. If you've ever had a stare-off with a roe deer you will know that they are pretty good at it. They will stay still staring at you sometimes for minutes on end, especially when they are on edge and a bit wary, which always makes it very difficult to move! But this male roe deer didn't seem at all bothered by my presence and popped his head back down to feed on the fresh green shoots of grass.

He looks quite old to me: his large antlers are fully formed and he has a big wet black nose – his fur is a little tatty but he's still in great condition. What a beautiful animal he is! I decide to edge a bit closer, pulling myself along the ground, supporting my body weight with one hand, holding my camera with the other, and as I do, he is walking closer towards me as well! Roe deer can be very flighty, and he knows I'm there. Every minute or so he raises his head to sniff the air and looks towards me. He can smell me but can't quite work out what I am because of the camouflage I'm wearing.

He is so close now that I decide to take some shots. It couldn't be a more perfect evening, with the light of dusk falling across the landscape and yellow flowers of escapee rapeseed sporadically dappling the field margins. And as he looks up, I hold my finger down on the shutter and take about 500 photos. But then, suddenly, he walks closer towards me, and decides to sit on the ground – directly in front of me! What is going on? I think to myself: this is a wild roe deer buck, and he has sat down right in front of me!? And as he does so he begins to ruminate. In much the same way as cows 'chew the cud', roe deer, being herbivorous ungulates, will eat vegetation and then bring part of it, consumed, back up from the stomach to chew again. And this roe deer buck is doing exactly that, not bothered by me being there at all!

I take about 500 more photos and shoot some video. The fact that he's sitting on the ground so close to me, not even blinking an eye – this has never happened to me before! This really is unheard of, and I can't quite believe it!

He stays with me for about 20 minutes until a noise from the valley startles some magpies and crows, which all take flight, whirling through the air making alarm calls. In a flash, the roe deer leaps up and into the dense scrub. I hear him bounding through it for about a minute, then it's back to silence.

I start to breathe like a normal human again and get myself up. I go to adjust the camera trap, which I hadn't put up properly given the roe deer turning up, but then decide to head home as the light is beginning to fade. As I walk through the fields, the sun sets over the North Atlantic and I cannot believe what an incredible wildlife encounter I've just had. One of the most beautiful and impressive wild mammals we have in the UK sat so close to me. I could have reached out and touched him. I'm so pleased that I took a gamble and sat in these fields last year. Even though my first visit was a little dodgy, they will always be one of my favourite places to sit along the field margins.

# SPRING'S GREAT ARRIVAL

It's 20 April at 6.30pm, and spring's abundant sights, smells and colours have truly arrived in Cornwall. As I walk downhill along a bumpy path that undulates underfoot, I stop and just look and listen for a moment. The path runs adjacent to a thick woodland, and the embankments leading up to the mature oaks are a thing of beauty. There are layers of deep green grasses, beaming with white greater stitchwort flowers that look like tiny fireworks, the occasional patch of forget-me-not and bobbing cowslip. As I look through to the edges of the woodland floor, I can see white wood anemones shining like scattered stars and the air has a slight smell of wild garlic. This early evening is warm and still – not an ounce of breeze in the air – and all I can hear is the buzzing of insects and birdsong.

As I stop and take it all in, I look down and see a patch of violets. Unsure if they are sweet or common dog violets, I bend down to have a smell – the easiest way to tell them apart. But I'm not greeted with the delightful, sweet aroma for which violets are famous, so I conclude that they must be common dog violets, which have no scent. The Irish have another word for the dog violet, 'salchuach', which translates as 'cuckoo's foot' and is very fitting for my wildlife find today. . .

With my head near to the ground, I see that surrounding the violets are red dead-nettles and a few black ants, busying themselves among the undergrowth. Although black ants are aggressive predators by nature, being formicine ants, they lack the ability to spray formic acid. This means that they can't sting and rely solely on their formidable jaws for defence and predation. Due to their size, however, they can't penetrate human skin and so cause us no harm. In fact, they are quite adorable.

As I'm enjoying this tranquil moment of serenity, being completely at one with nature, I hear a bounding towards me at full speed. The thundering steps get louder and louder, accompanied by heavy breathing. In that second, as I turn to look, an enormous creature has jumped on top of me, huge paws hitting my body and pushing me completely to the ground and onto my back, which is cushioned by my camera bag. 'Owww,' I say 'there's no need for that is there?' It's Isabelle, who has bought me back her ball. What a good girl.

I lie on the path looking up, Isabelle's long silly face now directly above mine, breathing all over me, staring into my eyes and looking incredibly pleased with herself. The ball's in her mouth as a large dangly bit of dog slobber falls right on my nose. I sit up and wipe it off with my sleeve as she sits there smiling. It's strange how our love for dogs is so great that even when we get their slobber all over us we still think they are the most wonderful beings on planet Earth. In fact, it makes us love them even more.

I pull myself up from the ground and throw the ball down the path for her again, and off she goes. This evening wasn't meant for proper wildlife spotting. Isabelle and I had just headed out to enjoy the beautiful spring evening, but, as always, I have my camera in my bag, just in case.

As we carry on down the path I hear the unmistakable and magnificent call of a chiffchaff – and what a beautiful call it is. I don't think there is one nature-loving person in the UK who doesn't get excited by the call of a chiffchaff, but they are very hard to photograph. At this time of year many of our spring migrant birds have already arrived or are imminent. And one group that completely changes the atmosphere outside are the warblers. This group is notoriously difficult to identify, given their size and behaviour. They continuously flit around searching for insects so they're hard to see, but when the air is filled with their different songs, you know that spring is here.

The chiffchaff does have a tendency to sing its delightful tune right at the top of the tallest trees and always seems to be just too far away to capture with my camera. I look up and can see this tiny olive-brown, fairly nondescript bird singing at the top of its voice. I know it is a chiffchaff, but I know I won't be able to photograph it, so I just enjoy the moment instead. At one time, chiffchaffs were only summer visitors, arriving here to breed each spring from their overwintering grounds of sub-Saharan Africa, or warmer climates in Europe such as Spain and Portugal. But as our climate has warmed, more and more of these little birds are overwintering in the UK and they can now be seen throughout the year, although they usually won't begin singing until the end of March.

As I stand and watch the chiffchaff, my mind is completely enthralled with the sound and I manage to take some shots as it swoops down onto some blackthorn blossom. It's as if, when you stand and really listen, every other bird song, insect buzz and even slight rustle in the undergrowth is all of a sudden incredibly loud. You become so in tune with the wildlife and environment around you that you forget where you are for a moment. And then, I hear it. No, I think, it can't be. It's a bird call that I haven't heard in many, many years, not since I was a little girl. A bird that is written about in storybooks and even Greek mythology. A two-syllable call that is the epitome of spring. It is none other than a cuckoo!

These remarkable birds embark on a 10,000-mile round trip each year. And it's a treacherous journey from their overwintering grounds of the Congo rainforest, with many perils along the way. Their numbers have drastically declined in the UK and they are now a red-listed species. Sadly, with over half of our cuckoo population disappearing in the last 25 years, their springtime song has become something of a rarity. Very little was known about our cuckoos' migration route and winter activities prior to 2011 when the British Trust for Ornithology (BTO) began their cuckoo tracking project. This has revealed much information about them and what could be contributing to their rapid decline.

Interestingly, the project has found that most birds that take their migration route over Spain not only have to travel an extra 932 miles, but that these are the birds that primarily breed in England, where they are declining the most. In one year, 2015, not a single cuckoo that took the Spanish route survived the trip. But the cuckoos that took their migration route over Italy had much better luck, with most surviving. The birds that take the Italian route, coincidently, are birds that come back to breed in Scotland and Wales, where cuckoo numbers are more stable. These, I must add, are just some 'Cliff's Notes' but I highly recommend having a read about BTO's cuckoo tracking project, as it offers some fascinating insights. The project also has a webpage updated regularly so you can see for yourself where the tagged birds currently are on their journeys.

The air is incredibly still this evening, so I can hear the male's famous call, but I have no idea where he is. It sounds as if he could be towards the bottom of the hill so I call Isabelle and start a brisk walk. The woodland alongside me ends at the bottom of the hill and opens up over a large boggy area, and I know that cuckoos like woodland edges so am hoping he's down there somewhere!

Cuckoos arrive in the UK traditionally on 14 April, and it is indeed around this time and the following week that they grace our shores with their presence. It is only the male that performs the famous 'coo-ckoo' call: the females sound completely different! I have only heard a female once and her call sounded very exotic – almost a cackling laugh – like something straight out of the Congolese jungles! The BTO's tracking project found that many of our cuckoos stay here for as little as six weeks, leaving again in June, which is a very fast turnaround to breed. But, being brood parasites, the adults of course don't have to stay.

The adults are famous for not raising their own young, instead laying their eggs in the nest of other birds (with meadow pipets, dunnocks, pied wagtails and reed warblers being among their favourite host species). The female cuckoos provide zero parental care and have nothing to do with the upbringing of their offspring, leaving it all to the host parents. Once the cuckoo egg hatches, the cuckoo chick proceeds to push all the other chicks and eggs out of the nest, so that the host parents have one job and one job only: to feed the young cuckoo! But of course cuckoos are substantially larger than the likes of a reed warbler, being about the size of a pigeon, and I'm sure some of you will have seen those almost monstrous photographs of a ginormous cuckoo chick being fed by their tiny host parents. They really are something else! It's thought that one of the reasons that brood parasitism evolved is that it allows brood parasites such as the cuckoo to put more energy into producing offspring instead of having to put vital resources into raising them. A female cuckoo in her six-week period in the UK can lay up to 25 eggs in different birds' nests, and she doesn't have to raise a single one!

As we come to the end of the path, I look along the old wooden fence that separates the woodland and the bog, squinting as I scan the area, which is now covered in shade from the trees. And then – I see him!! About 12 fence posts down from us is a male cuckoo! But, as soon as we see him, he stops his beautiful call and flies off down the treeline. I have zero experience filming or photographing cuckoos, but I get my camera ready just in case he comes back. Sadly, he doesn't, and I never see him again. I did go back each consecutive evening for the next week hoping that perhaps this was a breeding area for them, but maybe this cuckoo was just having a stop-off before heading elsewhere to breed.

Either way, it was still an incredible encounter, and the first time I had ever seen a cuckoo in Cornwall! And one thing now is for sure: spring's great arrival is upon us!

# PARROTS OF THE SEA

The skylark's song has to be one of the most beautiful and indeed one of the most famous songs of spring. As the males soar so high into the sky that they turn into tiny black dots you can barely see, you can still hear them singing their hearts out, as they broadcast their fitness to any potential female and ward off any rivals. As far as LBJs (little brown jobs, simply because many UK bird species are small and brown) go, the skylark must be one of the most impressive. The males don't have any fancy plumage to show off to the ladies, so they have evolved this behaviour of flying vertically up into the air, up to 300m (984ft), and will sing for as long and as loud as possible, with some males belting away for up to an hour. Not bad going for a small brown bird that weighs only around 38g (1⅜oz). Skylarks are birds that are highly associated with farmland, and they have suffered monumental declines across the UK, with numbers halving since the 1990s. This can be attributed to changes in farming practices as well as loss of habitat and resources. However, thanks to careful land management by conservation groups, these ground-nesting birds are plentiful around the North Cornwall coast, especially the location where I am today, as the air is filled with their incredible song. But the bird I have come to try to see on this coastal hike couldn't be more different than an LBJ. In fact, it is one of the most colourful birds we have in the UK. . .

This must be one of my favourite areas of the North Cornwall coast. On a warm April day like today, it really doesn't get much better. As I walk up over the brow of the fields from the National Trust car park, there are skylarks all around me and the occasional linnet. From where I am, I can look out over Port Quin Bay to the mesmerizing, almost turquoise blue ocean in the distance. The rugged coastal cliffs meander in both directions and the smell of sea salt hangs in the air as a kestrel hovers overhead.

It's around 12.30pm on a Sunday afternoon. Today I have decided to walk the circular route just north of Polzeath from Pentireglaze up around to the Rumps and around Pentire Point, one of the most spectacular viewpoints in the entire county. The Rumps is an old Iron Age hill fort and the area is steeped in history. Most famously, its name comes from its rock formation that leads down to the sea, as it has jagged rocky outcrops that make it look like a stegosaurus! What's even more spectacular about the natural grassland at this time of year is that the coast path is filled with primrose and bluebells. We associate bluebells with woodland, but they are abundant along the coast path, and, as I make my way out to the Rumps, there are bluebells starting to bloom and primrose as far as the eye can see against the backdrop of the ocean. Arguably, this is one of the most beautiful places in the whole of Cornwall.

But there is one bird in particular that I'm hoping to get a shot of today, either bobbing out on the open water or in flight, and to do so I have to head out to the very end of the Rumps in order to catch a glimpse of them. I know that they have already returned from spending the winter out at sea, so my fingers are crossed. I could be in luck.

I make my way past some ramblers and engage in some typical British small talk of 'lovely day for it isn't it' and 'apparently it's going to rain later', then head up towards the windy path that circles the north side of the Rumps. The coastal footpath is quite thin and near to the edge, and there are other routes that you can take, such as walking straight over the top of the brow, but I want to stay close to the edge and keep a lookout to sea. And as I turn the corner, I get a first sighting of the year – it's a male wheatear!

His magnificent blue cap and back, his pale yellow-cream chest and his smart black eye streak and wing make him stand out perfectly on the rugged green cliffside. Wheatears are ground-nesting birds that migrate to the UK each spring from their wintering grounds of Central Africa; they will arrive in March and April and stay with us until the autumn. The female will nest in rocky crevasses, old stone walls or old rabbit burrows, and they are a species that is abundant around the Cornish coast at this time of the year. I stop and try to take a shot, but he's too fast. To be fair, I wasn't ready at all, and I have one bird in particular on my mind, but it was still lovely to see my first wheatear of the year.

I climb up the cliffside to the far point of the Rumps and sit down to drink some water. If there's one thing about searching the North Cornwall coast for wildlife, it certainly keeps you fit! I set my camera up on my tripod and sit back and watch, with my eyes glued to a small uninhabited island that is right in front of me – an island that hosts one of the most abundant seabird colonies in the county. It's a true seabird city and at this time of year the rugged sides of this island are filled with razorbills, guillemots, fulmars, shags and cormorants. But Mouls island, which is its formal name, is also known locally by another name: Puffin Island.

Known to spend their winters out at sea, bobbing around together in groups known as 'puffin rafts', these incredible pint-sized seabirds have two breeding colonies in Cornwall. One is the Isles of Scilly and one is here, on Mouls island. Breeding pairs are monogamous and each year they return to the same nesting site that they had the year before. After breeding, the female will lay a single egg underground, usually making use of an old rabbit burrow. The young chicks are known as pufflings and will stay within the safety of their burrows for around the first six weeks, being fed by both parents. The adults feed their chicks on a diet of small fish and sand eels, which they dive under the water to catch and bring back to the puffling in abundance. Some sources state that a single adult has been recorded holding up to 83 sand eels in its beak, thanks to a specialized spiky tongue that helps them grasp their prey! The pufflings will stay in the burrow before venturing out to sea. But, when they are ready to fledge, they do this mostly at night to avoid predation by, for example, gulls, and, on this stretch of the coast, peregrine falcons.

I sit and watch the island and can hear the sheer noise made by all of the different seabirds. But given their size, and from where I'm sitting, the puffin has to be one of the hardest to spot. They have their burrows right on the top of Mouls island, so I direct my gaze there and wait, hoping to see a tiny flash of a glorious orange, red and yellow beak flying around. Their beaks are just astounding, and, in my opinion, are one of the best beaks in the natural world; they are even known to glow under UV light. We know that many birds have the ability to see in wavelengths invisible to the human eye, and it's thought that these glowing parts of the birds could have something to do with mate selection – maybe the brighter the glow, the more attractive the potential partner? As I've said, everything in nature has a reason, even if we humans don't fully understand it. So there will be a reason that the puffin's beak glows, as do the crown feathers of a blue tit and the feathers of a budgerigar. What makes this an even more credible hypothesis is that, during the winter, puffins completely shed their brightly coloured beaks, which leaves them with a dull grey-black one that looks as if they've dipped their faces in soot! In fact, during the winter months they look so different that for many years it was thought that they were a different species! So the incredible beaks they sport in the spring and summer must have some significance when it comes to breeding, most plausibly a signal of fitness and attractiveness.

'There's one!' I say under my breath, as I see not one, but two zoom towards the top of the island coming back from sea. Given their small size they are incredibly fast and can reach speeds of 55 miles per hour, and they can beat their wings 400 times per minute, which is very impressive for such dainty characters! From where I am, though, they are too far away – I was hoping to see some fly close towards the Rumps or be bobbing on the water just below. I sit for a good few hours and watch them whizzing around the island, which seems to have erupted into a hive of seabird activity, and I even watch a group of gannets diving beyond them out at sea.

We know that our seabirds in the UK have undergone enormous declines in recent years and continue to do so. Being highly susceptible to environmental changes, they have suffered greatly due to unsustainable fishing practices, lack of food resource, and climate change. Put all these things together with the recent catastrophe of avian influenza, which has ripped right through seabird populations across the UK, and our much-loved seabirds are disappearing. It is a total travesty.

As I sit and watch, I feel incredibly lucky to be able to look at a thriving seabird city, let alone puffins in flight. I didn't get any photographs of puffins on this hike, but I did go out a few weeks later with my great friends from Padstow Sealife Safaris (more on them later!) and managed to get a shot of a single puffin bobbing around on the water: a photograph I will treasure forever. They are such incredible and beautiful birds – birds that we must treasure and do whatever we can to protect for the future.

# May

# DOWN BY THE RIVER

May. The month when tiny cubs take their first steps above ground, fledglings start to appear along the hedgerows, owlets have their first look outside, and swallows promptly start their home improvements ready for the season ahead. It is one of the *most* glorious and enchanting months of the year. For a long time, autumn was my favourite season, with the changing of the leaves, the hedgerows filled with berries, the woodlands filled with auburn tones, and that crisp cold air greeting us for the first time in months like an old friend. Autumn is fuelled with magic. And don't get me wrong: I still love autumn. But over the years, as I have explored Cornwall more and more and become acquainted with my local wildlife, I must say that the month of May, and that of June, are undeniably my most favourite and all-consuming months of the year. Without any shadow of doubt – I simply adore them.

It's 5am on the first Saturday in May and I'm walking down a path surrounded by dense ancient woodland with the bubbling sound of a river flowing to my left. The towering oaks are now filled with their bright, fresh, green-lobed leaves, and the intensity of birdsong is so loud that it even dwarfs the sound of the water. Today is the day before one of the most celebrated in any birder's calendar. A day that sees people from around the world get up in the wee small hours of the morning to listen to nature's greatest symphony. Tomorrow is International Dawn Chorus Day: an event that is celebrated each year on the first Sunday in May and has its

A young fox cub growing up: the yellowy brown eyes
of a fox cub after the initial blue eyes at birth

A blue tit perched in a hedgerow
in early spring

A Cornish chough out
on a headland

Among the birch and oak: a tawny owlet before it sleeps

The perfect sea view: a delightful bunny
among the thrift overlooking the sea

A flock of oystercatchers on the rocky outcrops near Polly Joke beach

Flying lollipops: a long-tailed tit with nesting material in its beak

A pair of sea bunny kittens

A polecat taken using a DSLR camera trap at night

The elusive seabird: a puffin off Mouls island near Padstow

A northern gannet bobbing on
the water off Mouls island

The exotic-looking egret
on the Gannel estuary

Remarkable mimics: the winter Jay with its jewel-like
plumage imitates the call of other birds

A barn owl flying from afar
having caught a vole

The bright white chest of the
buzzard spotted with a kill

A bottle-nose dolphin leaping out of the water: one of the
most frequently sighted species of dolphin in Cornwall

Among the blackthorn blossom: the chiffchaff sings
its beautiful call from the top of the tallest trees

origins in the 1980s, from a place just south of Birmingham called Moseley Bog. But now it is celebrated by more than 80 countries around the world – and being out at 5am this morning I can see, or rather hear, why!

As I walk down the path the pre-dawners are already singing their delightful tunes. Robins, song thrush and blackbird are always the first to kick things off, and then, as the light begins to show, they are joined by our warblers and wrens. It is thought that birds sing at dawn in the breeding season because the sound travels further and there is less noise, with research finding that their song can travel up to 20 times as far at dawn as it does in the middle of the day, making this the best time for them to show off their fitness to any potential partners. It is also too dark to start foraging for food and they are less likely to be targeted by predators.

I carry on walking along the wooded path with my camera bag, as great tits, blue tits and wood pigeon add their voices to the early morning concert. I have come to this spot today to try to film a songbird, and it is a songbird that sings at any time of year and at any time of the day, and this fast-flowing rocky river is its perfect habitat. . .

I look across to my right and into the thick woodland awash with deep jades and light greens. The sun begins to rise as I turn the corner and see a carpet of violet-blues and purples lying straight before me. It stretches so far that it completely covers the ground, even up the far hillside: it is bluebell season!

These enchanting spring perennials bloom in the woodlands of the UK in their millions and are one of nature's greatest spectacles. They are also known as wood bells, fairy bells or fairy flowers, and there is nothing more magnificent than seeing an ancient woodland filled with these plants. The flowers where I'm walking are the native variety, of which the UK has around 50 per cent of the world's population. Sadly, they are now under threat by the Spanish bluebell, a flower that was first introduced to the UK in the 1700s as an ornamental plant species. The Spanish bluebell has a somewhat aggressive nature and can out-compete our native species for resources, such as space to grow and light to photosynthesize, and there is also the threat of hybridization. I know that these are native because of the smell that fills the air. If you want to identify which species you are walking among, note that the British bluebell has a sweet smell and a very distinctive droop to one side, whereas the Spanish bluebell lacks any scent and stands in the ground very upright.

I carry on walking for another 30 minutes or so in what can only be described as a fairy tale, a scene straight out of a story book: the air filled with birdsong in ancient woodland, bluebells as far as the eye can see, and the sun's first light reflecting off the babbling river. It's so perfect that it almost doesn't seem real!

I arrive at a bend in the river, a spot where I have a good view both upstream and down, and this is where I set up camp. On some trips here I have waited hour upon hour to see this bird, and as I take my camera out of my bag and set it up on my tripod, I take out an old jumper, placing it down on bare earth at the side of the path. I know that the species I want to photograph is here, as I've seen them and filmed them many times. This river stretches for miles, but these birds have an incredibly strong attachment to their territories, so if you've seen them somewhere before, you can pretty much put money on it that if you go back with your camera, they won't be far away! Typically, they have a range of around one and half miles, which is by no means huge, but it's still quite a distance to be walking up and down all day with camera equipment hoping to spot them. The best thing to do is to sit on my jumper and wait.

These birds have to be one of the most delightful in the UK and they are only found living along rivers and fast-flowing streams that are clean enough to support adequate insect life for them to eat. And when I say fast-flowing, I mean fast; they can often be found thriving in areas with rapids and white water and the Welsh even call them 'bird of the torrent'.

Their range in the UK spans from the north of Scotland, through Ireland, Wales, their stronghold in the north of England, all the way down to here in the southwest. And this time of the year is their breeding season. I know that some have nested along this exact stretch before and that they use the same nest site year on year. They have even been known to do so for generations, with one nest site reportedly having been used for as long as 123 years!

When it comes to building a nest these birds love rocky habitats and will often build their nests in the crevices of rocks, in old fallen trees along the riverbank, and even behind waterfalls. Breeding pairs are monogamous, and they will build small dome-shaped nests out of leaves, moss and any animal hair they can find. Their breeding season runs from March through to May, so right about now they will be very busy raising their young, which is perfect for photography as they *should* be making many trips up and down the river to catch aquatic insects to feed their hungry brood.

And then I hear it. In among the sound of the dawn chorus and the bubbling river, shining like liquid gold as the sun breaks through the woodland canopy, is the very distinctive high-pitched series of repeated scratchy notes whizzing towards me along the riverbank, getting louder by the second – it's a dipper!

The European white-throated dipper is the only aquatic songbird in the UK – and what a magnificent bird it is! It's a rotund little character, with a bright white chest and chocolate-brown plumage, lighter in colour on the head and with subtle auburn tones underneath, and is a wonderful sight along the riverbank.

In the dipper family there are four other species found around the world, all passerines, otherwise known as songbirds. They are most closely related to thrushes and get their name from their characteristic behaviour of perching on rocks and bobbing, or 'dipping', up and down. There are many theories about why they do this, and it has been found that they dip at different rates under different circumstances – sometimes up to 60 dips per minute! One theory is that dipping could help confuse potential predators about their whereabouts in the environment of fast-flowing water; another is that dipping could aid them in locating and focusing on their prey under the water through honing in on visual points on the riverbed (we see a sort of dipping behaviour in grey wagtails down by rivers as well when they are hunting prey). But it could also be for communication. Given the incredibly noisy and busy environment in which they live, dipping could be used as a visual tool for either defending territories or for courtship.

The bend in the river is perfect for my shot: right in front of me there are large rocks jutting out of the water. As I reach towards my camera, the dipper I heard earlier comes hurtling round the corner and lands on top of the largest rock right in the middle of the river! 'Perfect!' I whisper to myself, but as soon as I lock on with my camera, it dips a couple of times then dives straight under the water.

Out of more than 6,000 perching birds, also known as songbird species, found around the world, the five species of dipper are the only ones to use their wings to dive and swim underwater to hunt their prey. Despite being classed as songbirds they have many adaptations that make them perfectly suited for their semi-aquatic lifestyle. Firstly, they don't have webbed feet but have long legs and sharp claws that enable them to grasp the slippery rocks and stones on the riverbed and walk along it while they hunt. Yes – they can walk along the riverbed! To aid this they have solid bones to help counteract any buoyancy, an adaptation we see in the likes of common loons, puffins and penguins. Their feathers are incredibly dense, so they can withstand the cold, and their uropygial glands (preening glands) secrete an oil-like substance that they use to waterproof their feathers. Their uropygial glands are around ten times larger than in other songbirds of about the same size. They have incredibly strong wings that act more like paddles under the water, specialized nasal flaps that seal their airways, and a nictitating membrane that enables them to have their eyes open underwater. They also have higher concentrations of haemoglobin, which allows them to store more oxygen in their blood and therefore stay underwater for extended periods of time. They can go under for about 30 seconds, which doesn't sound long in the great scheme of things – but for a bird of their size it's an impressive feat!

I stay locked onto the rock where it had been sitting. I know from my experience of these fabulous birds that it is highly likely the dipper will emerge from the water with some sort of prey – either a mayfly nymph or a caddis fly larva. Right on cue, up it comes, swimming out of the fast-flowing water and walking effortlessly onto the rock with some sort of tasty aquatic invertebrate in its beak!

I hold my finger down on the shutter and take some shots as I watch it dip on the rock for about two minutes, twisting its body from side to side and standing tall. It looks almost pleased, its beak full of goodies. One thing about dippers is that they are very well-behaved subjects to film and photograph. It's like they got the memo in advance, and if you get them sitting on a rock, they always pose perfectly. And then off it goes, whizzing upstream, with tiny water droplets shining like tiny crystals still glistening on its waterproof feathers.

Very pleased with my shots, I head into bluebell-filled woodland to see what else I can find for the rest of the day. Dippers are one bird that I see quite frequently along this stretch, but every time I do it's still like the first time! They truly are like little rock stars, and I will never tire of seeing them down by the river.

# GHOSTS OF THE FIELD

It's 7pm on a Friday evening and the air is still. A male orange-tip butterfly with his striking white forewings and vivid orange wing edges takes off from a red campion, twirling up into the warm evening. Below me I see a deep iridescent metallic green insect with long antennae perched on a red clover trefoil leaf. I kneel down to take a closer look. It is a thick-legged flower beetle, next to an ox-eye daisy with two ladybirds walking up the tall stem. As I look closer, I see another insect, a shiny emerald green beetle ambling along like a tiny jade gemstone. It's a female dock beetle and she has her upper green wing cases raised because she is swollen with eggs. Just then a common carder bee buzzes over my head.

It's as if for a brief moment in time I have poked my head into another world; a jungle metropolis just a few feet away from us. It is busy, it is vibrant, and, most importantly, it is alive. It's a wildflower meadow.

Species-rich wildflower meadows are one of our most important habitats in the UK. They support a rich tapestry of life and play a fundamental role in our environment. It is nothing short of disastrous that we have lost 97 per cent of our wildflower meadows since the 1930s: not only do they support our pollinators, but in turn they are vital feeding grounds for our birds, bats and small mammals. In recent years, more awareness has been raised about their importance, and the need not only for their protection, but, where possible, their expansion. This is an uphill battle, but one that has been gaining traction. Even creating wildflower meadows in domestic gardens or outdoor spaces can contribute significantly in helping native plants and animals that are suffering across the UK due to loss of habitat, food supply and breeding grounds. No matter how minor we consider our actions in helping to provide habitat for species who no longer have somewhere to call home, it is never insignificant, believe me, not in the slightest.

The wildflower meadow where I am tonight, however, is carefully managed for conservation. It is not only outstandingly beautiful at this time of the year, but it is dense with vegetation and abundant with insect life, which makes this area the perfect habitat for the favourite prey of the species I have come to film.

Just on the outskirts of Newquay, this meadow is within walking distance of my house. Over the last few summers I have spent many evenings here watching roe deer in the fields, and I've even seen yellowhammers here. You might be thinking, why a Friday evening? Well, living in a party town I have found that Friday and Saturday nights are some of the best times to go out for wildlife photography if I'm headed to somewhere close to town. These fields are popular with dog walkers throughout the week, but on a Friday or a Saturday evening there is hardly anyone else around, which makes it even better for wildlife. So, while everyone else is in the pub, I take advantage and head out to the popular spots with my camera (although I do still make time for the pub – I just join when the sun's gone down!).

It is the first time this year I have come to the meadow in the evening hoping to film this species. Over the last few years, a pair have been nesting in a barn adjacent to the meadow. During the summer months, when they have been feeding their young, I have sat in this meadow and have had the best views of these birds I've ever had in my life, as they fly over the fields to hunt at dusk. But, given that this species is highly susceptible to environmental changes, and with our winters in Cornwall becoming more turbulent, I do come back every year and worry that one, or both of them, won't have survived the winter. When it comes to breeding, this species is often monogamous, although if one of the pair dies the other will find a new mate, or, if they haven't successfully bred together they will separate. Thankfully, for the last two consecutive years this breeding pair has always come back, and as the species nests in the same location year after year, I'm hopeful that I will see them, or at least one of them, tonight.

I walk a bit further down so that I'm directly in the middle of the meadow and sit down. As I take my camera out of my bag I look to my left and see a kestrel hovering and think to myself: well, that's a good sign! Kestrels hunt small mammals but voles are their favourite, so if a kestrel is hunting here that means that there must be a good supply of voles. As a rule, whenever I have gone out on a whim to try to find this species, I head to areas where I have seen kestrels in the daytime. The two species share the same food source so there's always a better chance of locating them at dawn and dusk. If you want to find wildlife, first you need to find what they are eating!

An hour and a half goes by and still no sign. A successful breeding season for this species is highly dependent on food availability: if there isn't enough, the female won't even lay eggs. Successful breeding and raising young also rely on weather conditions as these birds don't have waterproof feathers. In fact, if their feathers become waterlogged it can be deadly to them, so in times of prolonged rain they will avoid hunting, which can lead to starvation.

I sit there, in this glorious meadow surrounded by wildflowers as far as the eye can see, with the sun beginning to set, creating oranges and pinks in the sky. It is the most beautiful scene, but it's funny how, when you become invested in wildlife, especially wildlife you have filmed and photographed before, you can't help becoming attached to them one way or another: even though you're not supposed to it is very difficult to avoid. And, despite this incredibly gorgeous setting, all I can think about is whether or not they are still alive.

Just as I sit there despairing, I see a large shape out of the corner of my eye swoop over the brow of the hedge and into the next field. I quickly turn to look and it rises up again: the most delicate white plumage and a heart-shaped face, wings spread out in the evening sunlight as it hovers, with pure grace and elegance, in search of a vole. It is close enough for me to see the markings on its wings. I'm completely over the moon as I say out loud, 'Thank God for that!' One of the most magnificent birds we have in the UK is hunting right in front of me – a barn owl!

They are known for their remarkable hunting adaptions and there really is nothing like watching a barn owl quarter a field for prey. Their specialized wing feathers curve inward and have tiny hair-like structures that make them incredibly soft but also silent in flight, which enables the owl to hunt their prey stealthily. Their distinctive heart-shaped face, known as a facile disk, enables them to hone in on sound with incredible precision and funnel it through to the ears, which are just behind the eyes. Another incredible feature is that a barn owl's ears aren't the same height: one is higher than the other! This aids them in locating the exact position of their prey before striking.

I watch on as the owl elegantly twists and turns across the top of the wildflowers, occasionally dropping in an instant to the ground, disappearing out of view before rising back up again. It is hunting, but it hasn't caught a vole just yet. This is perfect for trying to get some action shots. I lock my camera onto the barn owl, trying to follow its every movement – but they are a lot faster than you might imagine when they hunt, especially when they drop to the ground. But it rises up once more and starts flying back to the barn, and it's taking the route directly towards me!

I swing my camera up to the side to get a shot. The sunset is directly in front, blinding me, so I can hardly see a thing, but in times like these I've worked out a method: just hold your finger down and hope for the best!

In a flash, the owl is back at the barn. I quickly look through my photos at the back of the camera and I got it! I got the shot! I'm absolutely elated! I stay for another 20 minutes or so then head back into town as the light is starting to fade. But what an incredible evening with one of the most superb species we have in the UK.

As I walk along the path, the sun having vanished over the horizon, I look over the wildflower meadow and think to myself what a special place it truly is. If only there were more places like this in the UK, brimming with pollinators, insects, small mammals, birds and barn owls. We simply cannot put a price on habitats like this – their value is without limit. And I hope that conservation efforts continue to preserve and protect our wildflower meadows so that our barn owls can thrive like they are supposed to – their ever-ethereal and magnificent presence, like ghosts of the fields.

# REAL LIFE MAGIC

When a wild species captures a person's heart it leaves them changed forever. A deep-rooted connection with the natural world is something that never leaves you. It becomes part of who you are, part of how you feel, part of your identity. You are enraged and cry when that species suffers and are beside yourself with joy when you see it thrive. It is almost a type of unrequited love, one that will never be reciprocated; well, not in terms of human love anyway. But it is more than repaid through the level of sheer fulfilment and joy that comes from simply seeing that species in its wild environment, seeing them flourish, raising young; seeing them safe. It is a love that will stay with you for the rest of your life. They become imprinted on your heart. They become a part of you.

It's late May, at 6.30pm. I sit among the tall grasses blowing in the slight breeze at the top of a steep valley. As I look out across open fields, with the ocean glistening to my right and dense woodland below, swallows swoop across the grass tips plucking insects out of the air. They are flying so close to me I could reach out and touch them and I hear a whitethroat singing its raspy call in the hedge next to me. I wait the entire year for this, for when I can try to photograph my favourite species.

But I'm not sitting here just to have a moment with nature. Lovely as it all is, I know that the species I want to film is in the fields opposite as I have followed this family now for many years. I'm mustering up the courage for what can possibly be described as my most hazardous wildlife venture – one that I do numerous times every year. At the bottom of this picturesque tranquil valley lies a treacherous and almost impenetrable bog, but crossing it is the only way to get to the fields that I want to film in. It is a total nightmare. Every. Single. Time.

After about 15 minutes of watching the swallows, and having a sharp word with myself, I begin my descent into the valley. When I reach the bottom of the hill I climb over an embankment into the thick hedgerow that runs along each side of the boggy marsh. Immediately, I have to get on my hands and knees to crawl across the wet muddy ground. The vegetation is so thick that it really is like being in the Amazonian jungles, not the north coast of Cornwall. But through years of trial and error, my wildlife buddy Dave and I have found this to be the most accessible route into the bog. I mean, I say accessible: it is still dodgy as hell!

I continue on my hands and knees for a few minutes until I reach an old willow. It's this old tree that plays a pivotal role in getting across. Below the willow is water – deep, deep water. We have prodded sticks all around this area before, all of which disappeared without trace. I have no idea how deep this section actually is, but I do feel that if I fell in, there's a high probability I wouldn't return. The willow has a single long-stretching branch that nearly reaches the other side of this deep section. So I clamber up onto this rickety old branch, my hands grasping the trunk, and walk precariously along, putting one foot carefully in front of the other to get as close to the end as possible. As I shimmy along the branch I'm nearly touching the water due to the weight of the camera equipment plus tripod on my back. I then hurl my body with ALL my strength as I jump off the willow branch into the air, closing my eyes and hoping for the best, but trusting that I've reached the other side of the water and gained more stable, though still boggy, ground.

Today was a good jump. I didn't even get wet feet!

I stand upright, my heart racing and my body shaking. I stop for a minute to pull myself together before traipsing across the waterlogged bog. I've found that following the paths made by roe deer in the more marsh-like meadow areas is the best way to cross, so I follow one of these. The somewhat traumatic journey aside, each time I reach the middle of this valley safely it's like stepping into another world. It's laden with bright yellow water iris, pink and mauve cuckoo flowers, and the first white frothy meadowsweet, which appear against a backdrop of bulrush. Pockets of marsh marigold dazzle underfoot and male banded demoiselles flutter in the air with their metallic green bodies reflecting the early evening light like streaks of glitter. This in itself was worth it!

After around a 15-minute trudge, I reach my next obstacle – a stream. In times of drought this stream is easy to walk across, but after heavy rain the water can come up above your waist. Today it's not too bad, at an average height, so once again, I get on my hands and knees to crawl through the surrounding undergrowth and stinging nettles. I then have to slide down the steep stream bank on my bum and get into the water, wading across carefully. One slip and I could ruin my camera.

I pull myself up the muddy bank on the other side and sit down on the ground. Finally, I say to myself, as I wipe the light dusting of sweat from my face and take a moment to collect myself. That part of the trip alone takes around 40 minutes, and I haven't climbed up this new side of the valley yet! But I'm now at the edge of the first field, a field in which I've undeniably had my most magical wildlife encounters.

I pull my ghillie suit out of my bag and put it on over my clothes before I move any further. I set up my camera on the tripod, knowing that from this moment on the species I want to film could appear from any corner of this first field. Fully camoed up, with just my eyes peeping out and my camera ready, I get on my hands and knees to peer through the undergrowth into the field. I can't see any fluffy red movements, just a few rabbits, so I decide to enter the field.

I walk up the side along the hedgerow, being as silent as I possibly can, with a new alertness about me. Everything is louder and my senses are heightened, as I know from past experience that at any moment I might have to drop to the ground and not make a movement if one should appear. Now at the top of the first field, I turn the corner and head down a muddy track for about a minute. This track leads into the second field, the field where the den is.

I emerge from the path and look out to the ocean that lies in front of me, scanning the second field that glistens golden, awash with buttercups. Nothing so far. 'Great!' I whisper sarcastically under my breath as I walk along the top brow and get into position. There is a distinct marking in the hedgerow in among the nettles and brambles where I sit most evenings when I come here. In my experience, *if* they come out of the den, this position will give me the best view, but it also allows me to scan each corner of the field. And then. . . the wait begins.

No word of a lie, I must have spent months in this field over the years waiting to catch a glimpse of this species. One day I came here at first light and sat in this field for 15 hours, and didn't even see one! They are highly elusive in rural environments, and nothing like their urban cousins. Rural and urban counterparts are now, in fact, so different that their skulls and snouts are changing shape; urban animals no longer need to hunt as they can rummage in bins and get fed Pedigree Chum from people's gardens. It's funny, you know. When I see videos on social media of people feeding the urban animals in their gardens, almost by hand, and taking photographs of them, I often think that they don't know how easy they've got it. They also don't have to cross a bog for 40 minutes!

It's now 8.30pm and still nobody, apart from a few summer chafers whizzing around my head. Dusk is around 8.40pm at this time of year, but given that I have to get back across the bog I have to leave in good time to allow enough light to see. There is no way I could even attempt to do that crossing in the dark, so I think to myself, I'll give it till 9pm. . .

But then I glance at my phone for the time and look up. Along the bottom edge of the field in among the buttercups I see a movement. It's a small creature about the same size as a rabbit, although I can't make out what it is, so I focus in on my camera. I wait another five minutes but there's nothing. Then, from the exact same spot, I see a pair of small black-tipped ears, a fluffy white chest and an auburn red back, so soft it looks almost like a ball of downy feathers. Two slate-blue eyes peer out from the hedgerow above a wet, black button nose. It then makes a little jump onto the field's edge as it chases a meadow brown butterfly, showing its bright pink tongue and whipping its white-tipped tail. It's a fox cub!

Overwhelmed with elation, excitement and joy I start to well up a bit. It is very difficult for me to put into words my love of red foxes. From my first-ever book, *Fantastic Mr Fox*, to my passion when I was little for *The Animals of Farthing Wood*, there is something about them that has captivated me my whole life.

I watch as the tiny woolly cub emerges further from the hedgerow, still so small, and I think that these must be some of its first steps above ground. Given its appearance, it must be around four weeks old, as the eyes are still bright blue and it has flecks of fluffy chocolate-brown fur still running through its coat. When fox cubs are born they have black-grey fur, which changes to a chocolate-brown colour at around two weeks. Then when they are roughly four weeks old their red fur starts to appear. When they are born, in the den underground, they weigh as little as 100g (3½oz). They are blind, deaf and unable to thermoregulate, and are completely reliant on their mothers for food, safety and warmth. For about the first two weeks of their lives they are even unable to have bowel movements on their own, so the mother will stimulate the cub by licking and nudging their rectal area, doing so during their first week as often as every two hours. Often the mother won't even leave the den until the cub has grown a thick enough layer of fur. The blue eyes are also a good indicator of a cub's age, as when they are around five to six weeks old pigment production will increase, turning the eyes to a yellowy brown colour.

I sit and watch, totally entranced by this tiny cub chasing the meadow brown butterfly, and then another one appears, then another, and then. . . another! A total of four fox cubs! Four totally wild rural fox cubs rolling around and chasing one another in the evening sunlight surrounded by buttercups. THIS is what it's all about – and in this moment the world completely stops. I don't think I've ever been happier!

I watch the cubs playing, pinning one another to the ground; one larger cub is being particularly boisterous with the others. This play may seem cute, but it is an integral part of their development, and even from this early age they are already honing the skills that they will need to hunt prey as adults. And then, from the hole in the hedge that I have always thought was the exact location of the den, I see a fully-grown fox emerge, with its luxurious fiery-red fur gleaming in the sunlight, with white chest glowing and eyes sparkling. It's Mummy.

She trots over to the cubs gracefully, almost as if she knows she's the queen of valley. For me, it's like seeing an old friend. I have followed this female for four years now, and each year she has successfully raised litters through to adulthood. She has a bushy coat and tail, and her eyes glint when they catch the light. She is a magnificent beauty, and looks like a fox you read about in storybooks.

Foxes on average live only to about three years old in the wild, but they can live until they are nine. Here, the valley is so cut off, there are no roads to cross, no poison being put out, the vile hunts are unable to reach the area due to its inaccessibility, and there is an ample wild food supply. These rural foxes are the healthiest I've ever laid eyes on, and I often think I might be the only human they've ever seen.

The cubs rush towards Mummy with a playfulness that is too adorable, and they jump all over her as she sits down. The boisterous one starts to frantically lick the corners of her mouth. The young are hoping that the adult will regurgitate some food for them, which is a common behaviour we see not only in foxes but in the entire dog family. Vixens start bringing cubs solid food when they are just three to four weeks old, despite them not having proper teeth until they are around six or seven weeks old, but the young will play with the food and lick it. The adults will also regurgitate food for the cubs to eat, and this is seemingly what this boisterous cub is hoping for, but it would appear that Mummy is having none of it. Both the male and the female fox play an active role in raising the cubs, and will continue provisioning them until they are around four months old.

The light is starting to fade, and I look down at my phone to see the time. 'Shit!' I whisper under my breath, the cubs and mum still rolling around on the ground along the bottom of the field. It's 9.15pm! I have to leave now, otherwise I could get myself into serious trouble trying to get back across the bog. There's no way I'll be able to navigate shimmying along the branch of the old willow in the dark while carrying all of my camera equipment!

So, as slowly and as carefully as possible – trying not to make a sound – I start to get into position to leave the field. Staying as low to the ground as possible, I begin to crouch walk, and yet Mummy glances over. But as I'm in full camo she doesn't appear fazed and continues to play with her cubs. I think she must be used to this strange moving bush by now but she knows that it is no threat, just a little bit odd.

I make it back down to the undergrowth by the bank of the stream in the first field and start to de-rig my camera and take off my ghillie suit. The last of the evening light is shining through the trees that tower over the water and clouds of midges dance. Despite the effort that it takes to get into these fields, it is without a doubt my most favourite time of the year. To see rural fox cubs and their mother thriving in the wild where they belong is nothing short of magnificent, and for me it's a childhood dream come true. Each and every year, it's real life magic.

# June

# THE 3AM CALL

The alarm goes off. It's 3am. I feel a slight cool breeze blowing through the open window and the first song of a single blackbird, a robin, and a thrush tinkle in the distance. It is almost too early for them as well, despite being among our earliest pre-dawn chorus singers. As I slowly open my eyes, I look out at the bright waning moon beaming down. June's supermoon is now past its best but it has been one of the biggest and brightest of the year. It is known as the strawberry moon, a name that comes from Native American tribes, because historically this is the time of year when wild strawberries are ready to harvest. The strawberry moon may be waning but it is all I need: a bright, still, clear pre-dawn.

As I fumble around getting ready, still more than half asleep, I simply go through the motions, almost on autopilot. I throw on some clothes, brush my teeth and pick up my camera bag. I had packed my bag the evening before, with everything charged and memory cards cleared, pre-empting my delirium the following morning. Most days I will get up at around 5am, but even for me 3am is pushing it.

Out of the door by 3.31am exactly, I begin the 20-minute walk to a medium-sized broadleaf woodland thicket nearby. Earlier on in the week I had a tip-off from a friend that a species I had only heard before in the wild, but never seen with my own eyes, had set up a territory in the thicket this year. Not only had the pair set up a territory, but they had also successfully bred.

Broadleaf woodland is the favoured habitat of this species, but they have started to become more and more adapted to our urban environments and are now often heard and seen in gardens and parklands, even in the likes of central London. Their territory size can span from 30 to 50 acres, depending on whether they have an ample food supply and a good-quality habitat. But given the size of some of our urban parklands, Hyde Park in London, for example, which spans 350 acres, such areas can offer this species a decent home, with an abundance of small mammal prey, as well as affording them the comfort of space. This demonstrates the importance of having ample green spaces within urban environments: not only do they act as important refuges and corridors for wildlife, but they also mitigate urban heat island effect (as green spaces can lower the overall temperature) and are highly beneficial for our wellbeing.

This is a species that is known to be highly territorial, sedentary and monogamous, with the adults defending their patch all through the year and not straying far from it. Knowing these behavioural traits makes me wonder how long this pair has been here. So often we have wildlife living among us in the smallest of spaces; they coexist with us under our noses, even thriving without us being aware of it. I feel that this is why wildlife watching, photography and film will never get dull, as truthfully, we never *really* know what's there or what we might find.

My thicket is in the middle of the town where I live, not a city by any means but still a surprising place for this species to set up home, given the unbroken countryside and thick surrounding woodland that they could have chosen instead. But perhaps their fellows put up too much of a defence while protecting their already-established territories so that this pair decided on a life in town.

As I arrive at the location it's approaching 4am. The herring gulls have started calling and their fluffy chicks, light grey with dappled black spots, are eagerly awaiting their first meal of the day. I watch them for a minute scrambling across the rooftops, almost shouting at their parents and pecking at their bright red beak patches in the hope of some food. About half a dozen weary revellers have been weaving and meandering their way through the near-empty streets, still clutching their half-drunk cider cans and beer bottles, with that look in their eye that says they don't want the night to end. I had expected to see more of them than this, to be honest, as half a dozen partygoers at 4am is tame for Newquay in mid-June.

The blue hour has started to fade and the sky is now a myriad of whites, oranges, pinks and greens as I make my way into the thicket and down an old winding unused and overgrown path. It's laden with stinging nettles and brambles with the first of their clustered pink and white flowers, so the walk through the thicket isn't the most pleasant. In my cheap leggings, now wafer-thin, I get continuously stung, but I reaffirm my refusal to buy new clothes until they fall apart. If I was barely awake before, I most certainly am now.

As I tussle through the undergrowth, I start to hear a distinctive high-pitched scratchy call directly above me. It is loud and repetitive, and is undeniably the begging call of the young that I had set out this morning to find. As I look straight up, with the first light peeping through the canopy of birch and oak, I find what I have been looking for. A tawny owlet.

I immediately drop to the ground, my heart pounding, which is what I always do when I find the species I'm after. The last thing I want to do is disturb them, so I try to obscure myself as much as possible. This is especially important for tawny owls as their eyesight is thought to be one hundred times better than our own in low-light conditions, and they are able to see prey scuttle along the woodland floor even in the pitch-dark. So when it comes to senses, the tawny owlet has mine beaten by a mile. In the half-light I unclip my tripod and pull my camera out of my bag, quickly setting up with my shaky excited hands. While I try to calm down and finally get my camera on the tripod, I glance across to another branch and, lo and behold, there is another owlet!

A female tawny owl will lay two to three eggs usually around late March when she will find a cavity in an old tree in which to raise her young. The eggs will hatch around a month later and the young owlets will perform a behaviour known as 'branching', whereby, before they fully fledge and start to fly, they will stay close to the nest but stand out on surrounding branches. This behaviour happens for a few weeks, but in fact tawny owlets will stay in their parents' territory until the autumn, which is when they are kicked out to go and find their own areas. Autumn in particular, then, is a good time to hear tawnies calling at night, as this is when the young are moving to set up their own territories. These young owlets above me are past the branching stage and already have most of their adult plumage but they will still be begging the parents for food at this juvenile stage. So if you do hear tawny owls calling at this time of year, chances are there will be owlets.

I've got my camera fully set up and am sitting surrounded by nettles, and the owlets have spotted me. So I stay completely still for a good ten minutes – hardly breathing and not making a sound. There's something quite astonishing about having two young owls staring you right in the eye at first light when no one else is around, the air so still you could hear a pin drop. It's as if nothing else in the world exists except you and them. People travel thousands of miles for wildlife experiences just like this, and here I am, at 4.30am, 20 minutes from my house in Cornwall.

They continue their begging calls and don't seem to be bothered by my presence, so I move my hands into position and focus on one of the owlets. But here comes the tricky part. How do you photograph an owl when you're still pretty much in darkness?

By using the slowest shutter speed possible, you can have the ISO at about 400 so your images won't look grainy. Of course, this technique risks a blurry image, but owls are generally still so are the perfect species to try this with. Not all of the pictures will be great – but after a bit of time and practice, I find this to be the best technique for photographing owls when it's dark.

I stayed with the young owlets until around 6am by which point their calls had stopped, and I watched them close their weary eyes as they went to roost, well hidden within the trees. As I watched the owlets fall asleep, the world around us was fully awake. Trucks and cars had already filled the surrounding roads on their way to work, and the early morning dog walkers had arrived, as had the early morning joggers. I garnered quite a few looks as I emerged back into civilization from the unused path, covered in dirt and with twigs and bits of grass in my hair. My feet hit the tarmac and I started the 20-minute walk back to my house. Little did these people know that I had just had one of the most magical wildlife experiences with a species that is rarely seen, right on our doorsteps. Well worth the 3am call.

# FAIRIES IN THE DUNES

It's 21 June. The summer solstice.

A day across the Northern Hemisphere that marks the peak of our sun's journey across the skies. An astronomical event that occurs as our Earth's axis tilts towards the sun creating the longest day and shortest night of the year. A wonder to behold.

Steeped in folklore, witchcraft, magic and mythology, it has been a point in the calendar that for thousands of years has been celebrated by ancient civilizations and cultures. If you have ever stayed up on midsummer's day to watch the sky, you'll know that the sun seems to stand still, hanging like a bright yellow fire in the warm air before it makes its descent over the horizon. The word solstice is derived from Latin, with the combining of 'sol', sun, and 'sistere', meaning to stand still. It is a pivotal day of the year, and one that is still celebrated to this day, with many people travelling far and wide to perform rituals and worship the sun's power, to rejoice in the enchanting change of seasons and in all of the mystical wonders it brings.

It is the perfect day, therefore, to look for fairies. . .

It's 9pm and I'm walking down a small sandy path holding my old tatty trainers in one hand and my phone in the other. I can feel the tiny white grains in between my toes, moulding to my feet with each step I take, bringing an overwhelming feeling of comfort and satisfaction. I look out across the ocean as it shimmers in the warm summer air; the smell of sea salt hangs on the breeze as I watch a single sand martin head back to roost. There is an ever-present golden glow all around as the marram grass and red fescue dance delicately as far as the eye can see alongside small, scattered patches of bright green Portland spurge that shine like tiny green exotic trees.

Tonight I have come to one of the most famous habitats found along the Cornish coast, one that tourists travel for miles to visit in order to relax and enjoy the immense beauty that this county has to offer. This midsummer's evening, I have come to the dunes.

Cornwall is home to some of the most magnificent sand dunes we have in the UK. They are like something from a holiday advert you see pop up on Instagram: soft, white and golden, sand nestled between the rugged headlands, abundant with wildflowers at this time of year. Sea rocket dapples the dunes with its tiny four-petal white flowers with their subtle hue of pink, along with sea bindweed, the latter always reminding me of marshmallows somehow, with their pink-purple round flowers streaked with white and their deep green leaves. This particular area is also home to plant species that grow only in dune systems, such as sea spurge, the rare Babington's leek and early gentian.

The sun will start to set tonight at around 9.20pm with the last light just after 10pm. It's the perfect time of day to be heading to the dune network, where, luckily, this species can be seen quite often during June and July. And you don't need a big camera to get some pretty amazing shots, just your phone will do! It's a species that dazzles and gleams under the night sky, a bioluminescent spectacle. In fact, they glow. . .

*

My first experience with species of the glowing variety was not on the North Cornwall coast at all, but in the depths of the

Brazilian Cerrado. The second-biggest biome in the country after the Amazon, and covering more than 20 per cent of the country's land mass, it is the largest tropical savanna found in Brazil. It's the land of the giant anteater with its two-foot tongue probing giant termite mounds, the maned wolf with its long spindly legs perfectly adapted for roaming the tall savanna grasslands, and the armadillo that scuttles along the ground as pumas lie in wait until dusk falls to hunt tapirs and pampas deer. Brazil is my home from home as it's where my father has lived for nearly 20 years, and it's a place that is entwined in my life and always will be.

I vividly remember one November evening being with my dad not long after he had moved there. We were out on his land, which is part of the *serra* (mountain range) in his area. November is the start of the rainy season and at this time of year Brazil has the most breathtaking thunder and lightning storms I have ever seen. And it's these warm wet Brazilian spring evenings that bring about the most ethereal and dreamlike display. As we stood in the warm moist air at around 11pm at night, we were surrounded by fireflies! This night was the first time I'd ever seen them, and Dad and I counted at least five different species flying all around us in their thousands – and when I say thousands, I mean literally thousands! Some were emitting fast flashing greens, others fast flashing whites. Some tiny ones twinkled like stars whereas larger ones were glowing a whitish yellow as they bumbled along. It has to be just the right conditions for nights like this to occur, when numerous firefly species fly around you as one. 'Breathtaking' doesn't even come close to describing such a night as this with the fireflies in Brazil. It was like a scene out of Avatar! I remember that one even landed on my arm and I watched it walk up towards my face still flashing its bright light. It was truly otherworldly.

\*

The time is now 10.30pm, so I turn on my phone torch and use it to navigate my way down the tiny paths in the Cornish sand dunes. I know these dunes like the back of my hand but I use my torch to guide me regardless as I don't want to damage any of the vegetation surrounding the paths. And within five minutes of walking I see my first one! Glowing iridescent green against the night sky, up high on a stalk of marram grass like a tiny gleaming jewel, it's a female glowworm!

When people think of UK wildlife, they very rarely think of glowworms, but they can be found across the UK right the way from Scotland to here in the southwest, although they become rarer the further north you travel. Despite their name, they aren't worms at all but a type of beetle, and if you go out in the middle of the night you can find them in hedgerows, along woodland edges and in grassland. It is the wingless females that glow brightly to try to attract a mate, a glow that occurs thanks to a type of chemical reaction when oxygen combined with a molecule called luciferin produces this heatless light from the lower segments of her body. What's interesting is that our glowworms are unable to control their oxygen supply as much as other species of firefly, so unlike the twinkling flashing fireflies in Brazil, our glowworms switch on their light for a couple of hours before switching it off again. The female lacks the ability to fly so she will climb to the highest most obvious point in her environment and wave her sustained light for a few hours to attract a male who can fly. This is very handy when you go out looking for them; if she's got her light on, she's usually in a really obvious spot!

I crouch down to take a closer look at this female as she waves her green-lit love lantern upwards in the air hoping to attract a male, clinging onto the highest point of marram grass. It's funny to think that she is related to the Avatar fireflies I saw with my dad in Brazil – a world away from the Cornish coast.

Beetles that glow all belong to the family *Lampyridae*. Over 2,000 species of these bioluminescent wonders have been formally identified around the world, but they are at their most diverse in the neotropics, where still very little is known about them. In 2022 three new species were discovered on the Amazon frontier, but given that the Cerrado is disappearing faster than the Amazon, we are potentially losing *Lampyridae* faster than they can be discovered. To add to that, we are not only losing species of the glowing variety, but losing all varieties of species, and probably faster than we can find them. Beetles are one of the most diverse lineages on the planet and make up roughly 40 per cent of all known insect species, with currently over 400,000 species formally identified, but it is estimated that there could be over one million. Yet with insect populations crashing around the globe due to continued pesticide usage, habitat loss, climate change and pollution, it does make me wonder if we will ever know just how many glowing wonders of the night there could be before they are forever lost. A travesty in itself.

She continues her light waggling and I look up. I can see five other females in the dunes all doing the exact same – an incredible sight! But after the female has mated, it's pretty much all over. Once the male has found the female's green love lantern they will mate and then the female will turn off her light, climb down to the ground to lay her eggs, and then she dies. But her luminous bottom-shaking efforts are not in vain, as one female can lay up to one hundred eggs! These eggs will take a few weeks to hatch and then the glowworm spends the next two to three years in this larvae stage, roaming around feeding on slugs and snails, which they will actively and furiously hunt. Once they've caught their prey, the glowworm delivers numerous bites laden with a type of toxin that liquifies their victim, turning it into a kind of slug or snail soup! Glowworms do all of their feeding during this larvae stage, and at the end of this cycle, the larvae will head to ground and pupate into adults. Once the adults emerge they don't even have mouthparts so do not eat and are only alive for a couple of weeks to do one thing and one thing only – to breed.

They are in an area where there is zero artificial light, and from where I'm sitting I can't see a single streetlight, any lights from any buildings – it is pitch black – exactly how it is at Dad's place in Brazil, and just how the glowworms and fireflies like it. Light pollution has been a massive contributing factor in the decline of this species, not just in the UK, but around the world. As I'm sure you can imagine, males get quite confused by all our artificial streetlights. Given that the adults are only alive for a short while, the males have to find the females fast. It is a huge race against time.

Streetlights haven't yet reached these sand dunes, nor where Dad is based in Brazil, and I hope they never do.

I'm so enthralled by watching these glittering female glowworms that I lose track of time. I look down at my phone. It's 11.45pm! I decide to leave them to it and start my walk back out of the dunes to head home. Seeing glowworms in the UK really is a must for any wildlife lover and they really are worth staying up for! The sand dunes on the North Cornwall coast are among the county's most valuable habitats, which is why they must be protected, respected and conserved for the future. They are also home to one of the most magnificent and magical species we have here in the UK, home to the fairies of the dunes. And if that's not worth protecting, I don't know what is.

# CLAMBERING CUBS

Pyramidal orchids have to be one of the most breathtaking flowers seen at this time of the year. Standing tall, reaching between 55cm (21¾in) and 60cm (23¾in), they are one of the most common orchid species in the UK. Their pink and purple clustered flower heads can be seen in meadows and along roadside verges and railway banks, and the field that lies directly in front of me this evening is peppered with them. On a closer look you can see that each of these clustered flower heads is made up of numerous individual flowers, up to one hundred on some spikes, all perfectly evolved with a ruched lip and an inviting spur to attract insects. It's a pollinator's dream and a true treasure to behold at this time of year.

It's early evening as I enter the meadow. I follow the path among the orchids and see hundreds of tiny, white, frothy, bubbly patches glinting in the evening sunlight. I remember seeing these with Grandma in Essex when I was little, and she told me that frogs made them while they walked through the grass. I thought this was actually true until I became interested in nature. Grandma was right insofar as 'frogs' made them. She just had the completely wrong type of frog and had left off the second half of their name. These tiny white patches of froth are made by froghopper nymphs, and they're also known as cuckoo spit because traditionally they appear when the first calls of the cuckoo can be heard. We have around ten species of froghopper in the UK, small jumping insects that are closely related to cicadas, and these frothy white balls are produced by the tiny nymphs during the summer months. The nymphs create these foamy fortresses around their tiny bodies by sucking the sap out of vegetation then blowing it out of their behinds, almost like an inbuilt bubble machine! And these wet foamy homes prevent the nymphs from becoming dehydrated, but also protect them from predation, helping them to avoid the likes of ants and stopping parasitic wasps from laying their eggs in them.

But I'm not here for the flowers or the bottom-bubble blowing insects. I'm here for one of my favourite species, and it's cub season. . .

I carry on along the path and through the meadow until I reach a dense thick hedge, an impenetrable mass of blackthorn and bramble entwined around one another, the surrounding ground laden with nettles, which are real stingers at this time of year. To any passer-by this would just look like a scrubby hedge, but I have followed this family for many years now and I know that this patch of scrub is full of wildlife delights! A quintessentially British species has made its home here: one that is famous for its love of woodland and for its stunning black and white coat, nocturnal habits, and its penchant for earthworms – one of the most marvellous species we have in the UK.

I found this family while camera-trapping the area a few years ago, and couldn't believe how active it was. I'm still unsure about how many live together in this scrub, but it seems to be getting busier year on year. The number of individuals that live together can vary for many reasons and is dependent on how good the resources, such as food and water availability, are in the area. On average between four and twelve will live together in a group, although up to twenty-three individuals have been recorded before and their underground homes can be hundreds of years old, used generation after generation.

Through trial and error I have found that the best way to film and photograph them is by sitting at the edge of the scrub, changing my position slightly each time depending on which way the wind is blowing. This species has an impeccable sense of smell that surpasses our own by some way. One whiff of you and they are off, so I will always change my position depending on the wind. But tonight it is still and warm; almost the perfect evening.

Water seeps through my leggings as I sit down on the ground. It has been raining the last few days, which makes it easier for this species to dig for earthworms – hence my coming here tonight to try to film them. They are most certainly creatures of habit. When I camera-trapped them before, their first appearance would be detected between 8pm and 8.10pm every single night for the two months I was following them. But weather can affect their activity patterns. If it has been very dry they may come out earlier to search for food, and this is often when people see them out during the day, because they are starving. In times of wet weather they will stick to their usual routine or come out slightly later, unless it has started to rain after a very dry spell, in which case they will come out a touch earlier to make the most of the damp ground. Activity patterns will of course vary across the UK depending on multiple factors: whether they are urban or rural, the time of year, and what other food sources are readily available to them. So this is just what I have found, after following this particular family.

This species is certainly hardy, not only in terms of ecology, in that they can thrive in many different environments, but also in terms of what they eat. Earthworms will make up the majority of their diet, but they also eat fruits, nuts, seeds, invertebrates and birds' eggs, and actively hunt small mammals, hedgehogs and waterbirds. And it's their ability to diversify in relation to their environment, as well as having a wide and varied diet, that has led to their success. We are fully aware that our environment is changing at a rapid pace, and, as our climate warms, there will certainly be winners and losers when it comes to wildlife. I do feel that this species will be able to persevere given its adaptability, as long as they aren't pointlessly wiped out by us first.

With my bottom now substantially wet from the soggy ground I take my camera out of my bag and look down at one of the well-worn muddy paths beside me to see a distinctive broad, five-toed paw print, the individual pads prominent in the moist mud, with four elongated claw marks at the front and a smaller claw print slightly to the side. 'That must have been made last night,' I whisper to myself. In front of me I can see numerous entrances into the scrub. One is a perfect example of a smeuse, a tunnel frequently used by wildlife – almost like a commuter path. Not only have I seen the species I'm after here but also foxes, stoats, polecats, rabbits and deer. It's a bit of a wildlife highway!

And then I hear it, a sound like no other found in the hedgerows of Cornwall. A distinctive chattering clicking sound is coming from the base of the scrub. The badgers are waking up!

I stay completely still, not even flinching as I hear the first ones busy themselves by the entrance to the sett. Usually it is the adults who emerge first, some heading straight off to forage while others begin their nightly chore of airing and changing their bedding. Badgers are impeccably clean animals and will air their bedding out to ensure they get rid of any parasites. They also won't bring any food back to the sett and go to the toilet elsewhere in what's called a latrine. Latrines are usually dug out around 20m (66ft) away from the main sett, and are a very handy way to tell if you have badgers living close by as you can easily find a latrine during the day!

I sit and wait, watching the adults rustling and snuffling at the base of the hedge, none poking their heads out, rather annoyingly for me. It's now gone 9.30pm so will be dark soon, and my camera won't be effective for much longer given the fading light. But then I see a small black and white striped face poke its little head out from one of the entrances. Small, fluffy, and round – it's a badger cub!

Most badger cubs are born between late January and early March in the UK, but here in Cornwall due to our warmer conditions some females have even been known to give birth in late December. Female badgers are known to undergo a process called delayed implantation, or embryonic diapause, a reproductive strategy whereby the female can mate throughout the year but will only become pregnant when the conditions are right, therefore increasing the survival rate of the cubs. This reproductive strategy can be seen in most other mustelids as well as in bears and marsupials, to name a few. The cubs will spend the first eight weeks of their lives in the safety of the sett underground, poking their heads out for the first time from around late April through to May. An average litter size will be between two and five cubs and they will be weaned by the time they are around twelve weeks old. By 15 weeks they'll forage for themselves. Come autumn, the cubs will be the same size as the adults and some will leave their natal sett to go and find their own territory, whereas others will stay within the family group. Being incredibly social animals, and the only badger species in the world to live in social groups, hierarchy and family bonds are extremely important to badgers. Dominant individuals will take priority when it comes to breeding and access to resources, but cooperative behaviour can be seen throughout the clan, with grooming and communication strengthening bonds and subordinate females helping to raise the dominant female's cubs.

I watch as this tiny black and white ball of fluff starts to emerge from the scrub, snuffling the ground as it goes. I turn my camera slowly towards it, but the light has now completely gone for any photography or filming. And as I switch my camera off, the cub is coming closer towards me, heading straight in my direction, with purpose.

I don't know what to do. This little creature is hurtling towards me unaware of my presence. Do I get up and leave or do I stay put hoping it decides to walk in a different direction? I don't want to frighten it, but it is getting incredibly close! It must not have smelt me yet or be aware that I'm here.

By this point the cub is within an arm's length of me. It has slowed down and is now bumbling along, but it is still headed straight for me, looking like it's going to sit on my lap!

Within a split second my senses kick in. As much as I would adore to have this darling little cub sit on my lap and to give it a cuddle, it is a wild animal and must stay fearful of humans. Sadly, not everyone in the UK wants to cuddle badgers. Many, given half the chance, would kill the lot of them. And in no way, shape or form do I want to be responsible for habituating this badger cub, even in the slightest, into thinking that approaching humans is a good thing to do, especially at this young age. It would, of course, be different if it was injured or had become separated from its family group and needed help. But this cub is in front of its house with all of its family here, and I do not want it taking my smell back to the sett. So I whip out my phone and turn on the video camera with the flash, hoping that it won't terrify the cub, but also that it will startle it enough to know that sitting on a random human's lap isn't the best idea.

The light shines in its eyes and it stops in its tracks, looking directly at me. It sniffs the air and works out that I'm a human, then almost does a roly-poly, jumps up, and does a circle before running back off into the scrub.

'Phew,' I whisper under my breath, as I pack my camera away and start to make a retreat across the field along the path. This was one of the most incredible wildlife encounters I have ever had, not just in the UK, but in the world. Having a wild badger cub that close to me was a dream come true, and to this day I still think about it and would have loved to have cuddled it. But when it comes to filming and photography, wildlife ethics must at all times be at the forefront of our minds. I want to be able to follow this family for many years to come and I want them to continue to thrive. So hopefully, in the future, I will have more experiences after dark with fluffy black and white clambering cubs.

# July

# STREAMERS OF THE SKIES

Animal migration is something that has fascinated and somewhat perplexed scientists and naturalists for thousands of years. In ancient Greece, the great philosopher Aristotle even pondered the mysterious disappearance of birds each year and tried to make sense of where they went, postulating that cuckoos transformed into either sparrowhawks or northern goshawks, and that redstarts changed into robins in the winter.

Our understanding of migration has of course come a long way over the last 2,500 years, and animal migration remains widely studied, revealing new insights year on year. It is recognized that the mass movement of species at certain times of the year is carried out as a survival strategy, one driven by numerous dynamic and complex factors, whether innate, learned or both, which can be triggered by environmental, climatic and behavioural changes. Yet the more we discover about the movement of species over vast distances the more we gasp, the more surprised we are, and the more admiration we have for the natural world. The Arctic tern makes roughly an 18,640-mile round trip annually, travelling from the Arctic Circle to the Antarctic Circle. Caribou herds travel around 2,000 miles between Canada and Alaska each year. Humpback whales travel as far as 5,000 miles across world oceans, and bar-tailed godwits travel more than 7,000 miles in eight days between Alaska and New Zealand, without even stopping. These journeys are undertaken across vast areas and demanding landscapes, yet each year species from across the animal kingdom, driven by their primal urge to survive, embark on these epic voyages, no matter what.

It's the first week of July and summer is now in full swing here in Cornwall. The towns are packed with tourists each day, so much so that you can hardly walk down the street. Partygoers fill the pubs and clubs each night and, because of traffic, the usual ten-minute drive to Morrisons takes what feels like two and a half days, if you're lucky. As I walk along the coast path behind the dune network that links Newquay to Crantock, I look down over the beach and my eye is met with the sight of brightly coloured windbreaks, beach towels, florescent bikinis and swim shorts as far as the eye can see, as the sound of screaming children fills the air, accompanied by the distinctive aroma of single-use barbecue charcoal and the occasional blast of music blaring from someone's sound system. Well, I say to myself, at least they seem to be having a good time.

I continue my walk along the craggy coast path and look over towards Pentire headland, which is packed with bright red poppies this time of year and is a conservation area for skylarks. I'm not heading to Crantock beach today to join in the summer merriment, but to my favourite and most reliable spot for filming one of our most marvellous summer migrants, a fabulous bird and the epitome of summer. It undertakes a migration of between 6,000 and 8,000 miles twice a year between the UK and South Africa in order to return to its natal breeding sites, covering as much as 200 miles every day at a sustained speed of around 20 miles per hour over a 6-week period. Not bad going for a bird that weighs around 19g (⅝oz)!

As I come to the end of this section of the coast path I'm walking right on the edge of the cliff face. A large seabird swoops down low across the top of my head, so close to my face that I feel the whoosh of air created by its wings as it glides along the air currents.

I look over the cliff edge and see the rugged grey stone cliff face dappled with green foliage and see hundreds of pairs of fulmars nesting along the ledges. I stop for a moment to watch as some of the adults swirl around in the air, gliding effortlessly and gracefully, and I see that the ledges are filled with hundreds of bright white bundles, small fluffy balls with tiny black beaks poking out and little black beady eyes. There are hundreds upon hundreds of fulmar chicks!

This fulmar colony is one I will visit numerous times every summer to film; from the coast path you can get some incredible shots of the chicks and the adults. Being pelagic, fulmars spend the majority of their time out at sea roaming the open oceans, only coming to land during the summer months in order to breed. Breeding pairs are monogamous, and they will return to the same breeding site year after year, with both the adults giving their single offspring parental care. Part of the seabird family known as tubenoses, they are, despite looking similar to gulls, in fact related to albatrosses, petrels and shearwaters. These tube-nosed seabirds are characterized by their nomadic pelagic behaviour, but also by a raised nasal passage on the bridge of their beaks, which houses a specialized gland enabling them to desalinate the sea water they ingest through their diet by spending most of the year out on the ocean. The higher nasal passage allows them to expel the salt from their bodies through the nostrils.

I have always thought that it's this tube-nosed feature that makes this family appealing, but of course, as we know, there is a reason for everything in nature – even if the result happens to make them look cute! But do beware of getting too close to a fulmar breeding colony: despite their endearing appearance fulmars produce an incredibly foul-smelling stomach oil that they will eject from their beaks at any sign of potential danger, the chicks being pretty quick to eject this on demand. (And this is where they get their name, from the

Old Norse words 'full' meaning foul, and 'mar' meaning gull.) It is nearly impossible to get the smell off your clothes!

It's now 6pm, so after watching the fulmars for a good 20 minutes I carry on off the coast path, just as it is coming to the perfect time of day. I look up and can already see them, my target for today's filming, whirling and weaving through the skies like little aerial acrobats, their sleek bodies elegantly twisting and turning along the breeze, helping them swoop at speed to catch insects on the wing with superb agility. Their delightful calls now fill the air – a much more welcome soundscape than the screaming children before. But this isn't the place to photograph them; they are far too high and fast. I'll have to get to the telegraph wires.

I know that the birds I want to film today nest in and around the houses and barns of Crantock village, possibly my favourite village in all of Cornwall. And these birds are known for congregating along telegraph wires in the early evenings of the summer months before they head to roost. Through experience, I know this to be the best way to get action shots of these fast-flying birds, as you can set up your camera while locked onto them as they perch on the wires and get shots of them when they take off. After spending time with these birds you instinctively know when they are about to fly – you can see it in their body language – and this is, for me, the almost fool-proof method of getting flight shots!

I head across a road and onto a grassy verge. This is my spot to film them. I have an excellent view of the telegraph wires coming from all angles, so I set up my camera and, just as I do, the first one lands directly on the wire in front of me, its long forked tail blowing delicately in the breeze. It has bright red cheeks and a glossy iridescent blue back, and its white chest glistens in the evening summer sun – a beautiful swallow!

Swallows are one of the three hirundine species that visit the UK each summer along with house martins and sand martins (swifts look similar in appearance and shape, but are part of a completely different family). Each year around April or May the first of the swallows appear in the UK for the breeding season, and most will return to the same nesting site every year. Females are said to prefer males with the most symmetrical tails, a sign, in a swallow's eyes, of good genes and fitness. And although the male and the female lack any obvious sexual dimorphism, the males' tail streamers are slightly longer. This is incredibly difficult to identify in flight, but if you see a group congregating along telegraph wires on a summer evening and manage to get a close look, you can sometimes tell male from female by looking at the tail length.

Their nests will be built under the eaves of barns, outbuildings and houses, constructed in an impressive cup shape and made out of wet mud and lined with feathers and grass. Breeding pairs will attempt two – sometimes three – broods each year, with clutch size on average being between three and five chicks. These chicks will be fed by both parents who will bring them numerous insects throughout the day. After around 22 days the chicks will fledge, but will stay close to the nest site and be provisioned by the adults often for a further 2 weeks before they have to fend for themselves.

As I watch the swallow perched on the wire, a few more join it, twittering and chattering to one another. And I think how incredible it is that such a small bird is able to make this vast migration each year.

Many species have a specialized protein located in the retina called cryptochrome, and this is one factor that scientists have found helps migratory species navigate their long journeys. Cryptochrome proteins are responsible for regulating the circadian rhythm in many species, but they also give some animals a superpower, providing them with the ability to sense or even see the Earth's magnetic field. It has been found that sea turtles, monarch butterflies, sharks, bees and many bird species (including swallows) who perform long migrations all possess these proteins, which can aid their navigation through detection of the Earth's magnetic field alongside the use of celestial cues from the stars and the sun.

There have been many stories generated about the disappearance of swallows during the winter months, and up until the 19th century it was even thought that they hibernated at the bottom of lakes, ponds and riverbeds, emerging from the muddy bottom once again in spring! Swallows swoop low over water bodies to drink and catch insects on the wing, so I guess you can see why people used to think, before we knew much about migration, that that's where they went during the winter. It was also suggested that they even went to the moon for the winter, which is ever so slightly more far-fetched!

There are about 12 swallows now all twittering away on the telegraph wires. A few at the far end are being a tad rowdy and I sense that they are about to take off. I lock my camera onto one bird in particular, with the fastest shutter speed the light will afford, and, as anticipated, in the blink of an eye four of them take off and I hold my finger down on the shutter, hoping to get one good photo at least.

I flick back through my photos and I'm pretty pleased with some, which doesn't always happen. Even though this method is the best I've found, getting a decent shot can still be pretty tricky. But this evening was a good one!

The light starts to fade so I decide to start walking back, the swallows still chirruping away among themselves. They are possibly my most favourite summer migrant bird that we have here in the UK: the streamers of the skies.

# A FLASH OF ORANGE
# AND BLUE

It's 9am and I'm walking alongside a meandering stream as a brimstone butterfly flutters across the path in front of me and skims my nose. Its pale yellow wings shine bright in the morning sunlight as it heads back into the alder buckthorn woodland to my right and perches on a leaf.

Brimstone butterflies always land on vegetation with their wings closed so that their pale yellow-green wings resemble leaves, perfectly camouflaging themselves against predators. It must have just emerged, I think to myself. The brimstone is one of our long-living butterflies, and the adults will live for up to a year, hibernating over the winter months in woodland and in among evergreen foliage. They can do this because they have a special type of antifreeze in their blood, and before hibernation they will also expel excess water. These two clever adaptations ensure that these beautiful butterflies don't freeze or succumb to the cold during our harshest months.

The hibernating adults will first emerge on warm spring days, sometimes as early as February here in Cornwall, and they are one of the welcome signs that spring is just around the corner. But across the UK we also see them in abundance during July as this is when the year's brood emerge as adults, and alder buckthorn, one of the caterpillar's favourite food sources, is where the adult female will lay her eggs. So this could be this brimstone's first few wing beats as an adult!

But there is no need for any clever antifreeze today: it's already 19°C (66°F)!

I watch the brimstone for a minute or so and then carry on down the dusty path adjacent to the stream. It has been so dry here the past two months, with only a light shower here and there. We are in desperate need of a deluge but, unfortunately, it doesn't look like one is on the way.

Terrifyingly, these spells of drought are becoming longer and hotter each year: reservoirs are drying up, uncontrollable mass fires are destroying precious habitat and wildlife, and water scarcity is an increasing issue. But in the UK, we are currently seeing only the marginal effects of climate change. It has been, and continues to be, indisputably far more devastating and catastrophic in the global south. This is not, however, a book about the climate crisis and the accompanying eco-anxiety, nor is it about the shameful and hypocritical actions of the global north towards both our changing climate and the communities in the global south – there are other authors, activists and books for that. But these continued dry spells and the rising heat – and what they mean for our wildlife and the human race – ought to be acknowledged, each and every day.

I have come to this stretch of stream because I know that this is the perfect time of year to photograph and film one of the most elusive bird species in the UK. The adult's first broods should have fledged their tunnel nests and be flying up and down the water's edge, sometimes in small groups. Regarded as notoriously difficult even to see, these birds are a bit of wildlife filmmaker's bucket-list species and, through experience, I've found that the fledglings aren't as flighty as the adults, and can often be easier to film. I know this area like the back of my hand and am aware that at least three pairs nest along this stretch of water. In previous years I have seen many fledglings flying up and down along the water's edge.

Each adult breeding pair will have a specific territory that will range from around two-thirds of a mile up to three miles. A pair can have up to three broods each breeding season, and each clutch can contain between five and seven eggs, which means my chances of filming a fledgling today are pretty high. It is also the perfect time of year. But with wildlife, as we know, nothing is ever certain – no matter how good your odds!

I walk along the path, the dappled sunlight coming through the trees, and pass an old willow tree. There is a bend in the river, and, over thousands of years, the weather, root networks, and the highs and lows of the stream have created the almost perfect natural seat on the grassy embankment. I have sat on this seat for hours, if not days, waiting to try to photograph this species. It's my little secret nature chair. When I'm here on my own for hours on end, I often wonder what stories this bend in the river could tell, as I know I can't be the first and only person to sit here.

I take my camera out of my bag, attach it to my tripod and drink some water. Even though I'm pretty much in the shade, thanks to the tree canopy, it is still incredibly warm and is getting hotter by the hour. Thankfully, there is a small breeze coming down the watercourse, which is taking the edge off the midsummer sun.

I wait for about an hour and half, seeing only a couple of mallard ducks and a rowdy moorhen that seems to want the entire surrounding area to know that he's here. But then I hear it! That undeniably distinctive high-pitched 'seet-seet' call, repeated in rapid succession. It's sharp, an almost tinny sound, that carries far and wide along the river's edge. I can hear that it's whizzing along the stream's edge, coming right in my direction. I get into position, readying my hands on my camera, hoping to get an action shot as I have a clear view downstream from where the call is hurtling.

But then... in a split second... it's all over. It felt like as soon as I saw it, it disappeared upstream! A magnificent kingfisher!

It was going so fast that I couldn't tell if it was a juvenile, a male or a female. It was just a flash of orange and blue, tearing down the river and off round the corner!

Around the world there are over one hundred different species of kingfisher and they can be found on nearly all continents, with most species distributed within tropical regions. Here in the UK we have only one species, *Alcedo atthis*, and they are present along waterways throughout the country. They lack any true sexual dimorphism so it can be difficult to tell male and female kingfishers apart, especially when they come bombing past you at 25 miles per hour. They are also a lot smaller than you might imagine, a mere 19cm (7½in) in length with a wingspan of around 25cm (9¾in) and weighing in at just 34g (1¼oz) to 46g (1⅝oz), making it even harder. But a tell-tale sign, and the easiest way to sex a kingfisher, is to look at the lower mandible of the beak: in the males this will be jet black, whereas in the females it will be orange. Kingfisher fledglings, on the other hand, are very tricky to sex, as they won't develop their full adult beak colouration until they are roughly a year old.

Famed for their impeccable precision when hunting, they have the ability to stay completely still, perched on a nearby branch or bulrush, and to focus their eyesight on tiny fish beneath the water, before diving down at lightning speed, striking with faultless accuracy. Kingfishers have the ability to see in binocular vision when submerged in the water because of their two foveae, the area of the eye that has the highest density of photoreceptors, allowing more light into their eyes. They also have a nictitating membrane and water-repellent plumage. They keep their bodies streamlined as they enter the water and will then open their wings to reduce drag. True masters within their environment. They are so well designed that the kingfisher was the inspiration and model for the Japanese bullet train!

I must add, though, that if you have encountered in-flight dive shots of kingfishers, or images of them diving under the water to catch their prey, be aware of the ethics of such photography. These shots became popular some years ago but the way they are captured is truly hideous. It was discovered that photographers would fill a glass or Perspex box with minnows (one of the kingfisher's prime food sources) and place it directly under a makeshift perch in an area that kingfishers were known to frequent. The birds would be attracted to the pool of fish and dive into the water to catch them. But hitting the water at 25 miles per hour would lead many birds to hit the bottom of the box, break their necks and die.

I remember when I first saw a selection of what I initially thought were incredible photographs, only to find out that the series featured five different kingfishers, all of whom were led to their deaths, just for someone to get 'likes', followers or clout. Disgusting, abhorrent and disgraceful. This has led me to look at every wildlife photo and ask the question: 'How did they get this?' And highly unethical wildlife photography and filming is on the increase. There has been a rise in 'photography game farms', particularly in North America, whereby foxes, lynx, bears, wolves and pumas, to name just a few, are kept in appalling conditions and let out of their tiny cages only when 'wildlife photographers' pay to take some shots. This can be attributed to the rise in social media and to people wanting to be

'Instagram famous' – but they do not care about wildlife, not one little bit.

That said, there are of course some brilliant photographers who keep ethics at the forefront of what they do and who will wait for weeks and months to get the perfect shot. These people must be celebrated. But when you see a photograph that is almost too perfect, always question how it was achieved.

I look over across the stream to an old fallen branch and I hear in the distance another kingfisher getting closer to me by the second as it races down the stream. 'This could be it!' I whisper to myself as I line up my camera, focused on the fallen branch. I have seen kingfishers using this natural perch before, so I'm hopeful that one may land here today.

Then it appears, with that iridescent azure plumage, the bright orange chest with white patches, and it lands on the branch! With a fish in its beak!

I hold my finger down on the trigger and take as many shots as possible, hoping that at least one is in focus, before the bird takes off and heads upstream! I can hardly breathe!

I look back through my photographs, and while they aren't the best, it is still a kingfisher – possibly the most colourful and awe-striking bird we have in the UK! But their famous colours are actually a trick of the light. Vertebrates struggle to produce the pigment blue and most of the blue we see in nature is due to what's known as structural colouration. The turquoise, teal and blue we see in many species are produced by the nano-like structures of the feathers, which absorb, reflect and diffract different wavelengths of light in such a way as to appear blue in colour. We see this in the scales of butterflies, some insect species, and in tropical fish. A peacock's tail feathers are brown, sadly, and the kingfisher's feathers a brown-grey. I remember being sorely disappointed when I found this out, but then realized how utterly incredible the natural world is. Structural colouration in different species has evolved for a multitude of reasons and it can often look different at varying stages in the life cycle of a species. Yet another wonder of the natural world!

I look at my phone and the time is 3pm. I'm not entirely sure where the last six hours have gone but I decide to head back home; soon it will be Isabelle's walk and dinner time. It has been an incredible day down at the stream and although my photographs aren't the best, I'm ecstatic to have got some all the same. Plus, I have taken them naturally and haven't used an awful box or staging – something that I would never do in a million years. Kingfishers are one of the hardest species in the UK to photograph, because of their speed, size and habitat, but they should always be photographed ethically and respectively, even if all you see at first is a flash of orange and blue.

# A LAND THAT TIME FORGOT

My old muddy boots step into the dew-kissed grass. Tall, slender, deep green vibrant shoots stretch as far as the eye can see, glistening like diamonds as the dappled evening sunlight beams onto the open meadow through the surrounding trees. And with every step I must take extra care, as I'm greeted by hundreds of hopping emerald gems, minuscule amphibians no larger than my fingertip that twinkle with each leap, scattering themselves in among the safety of the long grass. Below my feet the earth is full of hundreds of baby froglets! And when I say hundreds, I mean hundreds! To this day, I have never been anywhere else in the UK where I have seen froglets in abundance like this, their smooth mottled skin making them perfectly camouflaged within the undergrowth, only becoming apparent as they take what must be some of their first wary leaps into the unknown wilderness. As I make my way through the meadow towards the margins of damp woodland, a male broad-bodied chaser whizzes past my ear with a gentle humming as I catch a flash of the pale dusty blue tapering down his abdomen and I hear blackcap, wood warblers and chaffinch trilling their delightful tunes in the adjacent hedgerows as common lacewings dance in the still air.

Welcome to the land that time forgot.

Every time I come to this place the biodiversity is simply alive, no matter what time of day and no matter the season. The ecosystem regeneration that has happened here over the past few years in this landlocked pocket of Cornwall is quite extraordinary. As this area has revived, a ripple effect has occurred, spilling out into the surrounding landscape, providing cleaner air, more native plants, an abundance of wildlife and improved water quality. Willow tits, our fastest declining resident bird, have now been seen here. They rely on stands of decaying wood in which to nest and make their homes among the damp and wet woodland. Polecats, water rail, merlin and 11 species of bat are just some of the species that now frequent this area. And as for the trout – since the regeneration project they have doubled in size! An area of farmland has been transformed right before our very eyes into something otherworldly. And what is even more extraordinary is how quickly this has occurred – just a few short years. This is clear, tangible evidence of rewilding in action, and no one can deny the proof of concept: the difference is like day and night.

I make my way out of the damp meadow and across a muddy bank. My hands touch the metal gate and a sharp, icy feeling rushes through my fingers as I open it, making sure that it's firmly closed behind me, mainly because the species that now lives in this wild enclosure has a bit of a reputation as an escape artist! As I move ahead it is like stepping into another world, or going back in time. I'm surrounded by coppiced broadleaf trees, varying in their twisted shapes and sizes, all completely different, like singular artist sculptures. You can see clearly that some trees have been gnawed, other trees are now held up by just a thin piece of remaining trunk, and some, with distinctive teeth marks, have a clear and perfectly rounded stump that have been gnawed into a characteristic sharp point. Hundreds of perfectly curled wood chippings cover the ground, some an old weathered dark brown, but some still bright creamy orange. I pick up a fresh cream-coloured chip and feel the texture between my fingers, that coarse scratchy feeling of wood, but I can also feel the teeth marks. It's as if I can feel each individual cut that was used to fell the tree itself. 'This was done last night, they must be doing some home improvements,' I whisper to myself as I look out to the first lodge. I am, of course, at the Cornwall Beaver Project.

On 16 June 2017 an ambitious project was started by possibly two of my favourite people in the entire county, Chris and Janet Jones, some of the most forward-thinking farmers I have ever had the pleasure to meet, and whom I am now privileged to call my great friends. Not only are they ardent conservationists, but they are two of the most hardworking people I know. They are also hilariously funny. I have spent many an hour with them at this project in fits of giggles while waiting around, and it is always a total joy to visit them, even if we don't see any beavers. And, when it comes to farming and conservation going hand in hand, I wish there were more people like Chris and Janet. They farm organically, with landscape and biodiversity health always at the forefront of everything they do. If more farms were run the way they do it, perhaps we wouldn't be in such an ecological crisis. . . but those are thoughts for a different book altogether.

After years of flooding in the village of Laddock, Chris decided that he would try introducing beavers to slow the watercourse that left his land. And, in partnership with Cornwall Wildlife Trust and Exeter University, two beavers were introduced into a five-acre wild enclosure, where they began work immediately creating their lodges, dams and ponds. That's one thing about beavers: they are always busy! And it's this wetland creation that dramatically changes the landscape and provides homes for, and significantly increases, biodiversity, which is why beavers are known as ecosystem engineers and a keystone species.

Beavers are famous for their ability to reduce and prevent floods, as their dams and ponds hold water back and inhibit flooding downstream. These beaver ponds can also help in times of drought by acting as natural reservoirs. They filter out harmful pollutants, including agriculture chemicals, making the water cleaner, and by increasing carbon capture they are also hugely beneficial in the fight against climate change. So all in all, having beavers is simply a win-win!

Absent from the great British countryside for over 400 years, this large mammal, in fact the largest rodent in Europe, has started to make a comeback here in Britain, thanks to immensely dedicated conservationists and ecologists. Yet our history with beavers is a murky one: by the 16th century we had exterminated these gentle giant herbivores to the point of extinction. And this wasn't just the sorry state of affairs in Britain, but also the story across much of mainland Europe. These animals are endlessly hunted for their thick warm fur, their meat and their castoreum, a pungent thick liquid that is secreted from the beaver's anal glands and is what they use to mark their territories. This secretion smells (and apparently tastes) very similar to vanilla and was used in perfumes as well as in foods as a 'natural flavouring' – although personally, I'd much rather have actual vanilla pods flavour my food than a beaver's anal gland secretions. . .

The time now at the Cornwall Beaver Project is just gone 8pm, as I take my camera out of my bag and set up at the side of the first pond in front of the lodge. The main lodge is the first that this pair built when they arrived, and it really is like something out of a storybook! It almost doesn't seem real!

Since their arrival the beavers have completely transformed this once-straight stream into a complex and abundant mosaic of wetlands, ponds and streams encompassing the entire floodplain, and have also built eight new dams. Beavers build these structures as a form of safety, behaving still as if they live in a landscape where bears and wolves roam. By establishing these vast networks of wetlands and channels, they can quickly jump into the safety of the water should a potential predator be nearby. I just hope that no one tips them off that they are now living in a landscape without bears and wolves. I wonder if they would still go to all of this architectural effort if they knew that. . .

I like to sit by this main lodge as I know that there is at least one underwater entrance to the lodge near here. You can pretty much guarantee that if you sit long enough one animal will pop up in the water having emerged ready for its nightly activities. Beavers are mainly nocturnal, but their crepuscular activities make them quite easy to spot if you know where to look. So, I sit and wait.

Then, about 20 minutes later, I spot my first bubbles! Beaver bubbles!

Being semi-aquatic mammals, beavers are perfectly adapted for life in the water. They can hold their breath for up to 15 minutes, have a nictitating membrane that enables them to have their eyes open underwater, and can swim up to five miles per hour using their webbed feet and flat wide tail to help propel them through the water. Their impressive tails aren't just to aid swimming but also store fat reserves that help them through the cold winter months, and they use their tails a lot in communication. If you come across a beaver and see or hear the tail slapping on the water, they'll be doing so, having sensed danger, to alert others of potential threat. It is also a sign of aggression. Beavers are herbivores and totally harmless, but if you do encounter tail slapping it's best to move away, as it means that your presence is making the beaver uncomfortable.

I follow the bubbles with my camera as I know that a beaver will pop its head up any second. When they are cruising along under the water I can't tell a male from a female, but I will be able to tell a kit due to its size. Just a year after the adults were introduced to the pond they bred successfully, having two kits. The first baby beavers to be born in Cornwall in over 400 years! Since then they have successfully bred again, which is a wonder in itself. I often think just how incredible it is to have beavers living down the road from me: being a mammal girl at heart, and seeing that we've extirpated most of our large mammals, having beavers back is just wonderful!

And then I see two beady black eyes and a black shiny nose pop out from below the water, surrounded by a mass of soft, light-brown fur, as the beaver slowly travels through the water around the main lodge then heads back towards it. Yes! I think to myself, it's going to come on shore to feed!

Then, as if it has heard me, the beaver gently pulls itself from the water's edge and onto the embankment of the lodge and starts to pick vegetation to eat, precisely picking the most appetizing parts. I hold my camera steady and take some shots of the large adult. That is one good thing about beavers. If they do come on land to feed they are very good subjects as they will stay pretty still for quite a while as they have their breakfast.

After around 15 minutes of feeding, the beaver slides back into the pond, swimming down to the other end and over a small embankment that takes you into the other part of their wetland area. Now the light is beginning to fade so I decide to pack up and head off before it is pitch black.

As I walk out past the main lodge, which looks like a fairy tale, I imagine what old Cornwall must have been like, hundreds if not thousands of years ago, when the landscape was relatively untouched and still wild, peppered with vast wetland habitats surrounded by continuous dense woodland filled with bears, bison, wolves, lynx and beavers. Just having beavers here transports your mind to a time in nature when our ecosystems were fuller and more abundant. And I do hope that one day, at least in certain parts of the UK, we can get back to this, and the land that time forgot will not be forgotten any more.

# August

# SEA BUNNIES

Straight in front of me I see a silhouette. Effortlessly soaring high, it weaves in and out of sight, slightly obscured by the early evening glow as the bright August sun starts to make its descent down across the ocean's horizon. Moving along the jagged cliffs of the North Cornwall coast, it is one of the most distinguishable falcon silhouettes in the raptor family, with its long, wide pointed wings, its short square tail and its broad head. It is too far away to make out its feather plumage, but I know by the way it is moving and by its habitat and stature that it is none other than the fastest bird in the world. In fact, it is the fastest animal to ever live on planet Earth, reaching top speeds of 240 miles per hour when it stoops mid-flight for its avian prey. It is a magnificent peregrine falcon.

We are very lucky here in Cornwall to see peregrine falcons along the coastal cliffs quite frequently, but each and every time is a total privilege. As a raptor species, they make their home on the sea cliff faces and in among the craggy crevices, which make for an excellent nesting habitat. These towering cliffs with their panoramic views also give them the advantage of height, as they can sit in wait of any unsuspecting prey. And it is this hunting behaviour that has made them so successful in urban areas. Given the number of feral pigeons, ducks and starlings that now live in our towns and cities, peregrines have an abundant food supply, and many have swapped the rugged cliff faces for skyscrapers. A 2019 study found that peregrines in urban areas (one of our most successful urban bird species in the world) are now more successful than are their rural counterparts. Another study found that peregrines are even adapting to hunting at night in urban areas, utilizing artificial streetlights to hunt under the cover of darkness, predating species such as moorhen, teal and water rail, and even nocturnal migrants such as woodcock!

As awe-inspiring a sight as it is, it is too far away to get any shots, though I stop for a moment to take in its magnificence before it disappears down the coast and finally out of view. And I'm not on the coast path this evening for peregrines. I'm here for one of my favourite and most reliable species, and it is both the perfect time of year and time of day for them.

I walk along the South West Coast Path out past Polly Joke beach heading towards Holywell Bay and see some grey seals bobbing about in the water below. The raspy sound of stonechats fills the air, along with skylarks up above and oystercatchers in the distance, with their distinctive peep-peeping call echoing around the rocky outcrops below. I might be slightly biased given that I live here, but when the weather is just right in midsummer, there is nowhere in the world I would rather be. It really is perfect place for any lover of the natural world.

I carry on up and around the corner, and the pink sea thrift, though now past its best, still carpets the ground along this part of the coast path as far as the eye can see, like a world of pink-white fluffy stars. I stop and do a double take at one patch, having just caught a flash of black and deep red. I instantly get down on my hands and knees. It is a beautiful six-spot burnet moth resting among the sea thrift.

These colourful, medium-sized day-flying moths are abundant along the North Cornwall coast at this time of year. They have a red and black colouration to ward off potential predators, as, despite their attractive appearance, these moths have a feature that can be deadly to any bird that might attempt to catch them. They produce hydrogen cyanide, which not only makes them unpalatable – a predator would most likely spit the moth out if it caught one – but in large amounts could kill. The caterpillars feed on bird's-foot trefoil and are able to assimilate the toxins in the plant's leaves to produce hydrogen cyanide, but they are also able to produce it themselves. The six-spot burnet moth is poisonous at every stage of its life cycle, which is a pretty clever evolutionary adaptation for a moth that flies during the day when predator activity is at its highest.

I watch as it climbs up the sea thrift, then spreads its wings and bumbles off into the distance. The sun is getting lower in the sky now, which means the perfect filming conditions, so I carry on to my spot – the warren of dreams!

All along this stretch of coast, high on top of the cliff edges, rabbits have made their homes. There are vast networks of underground tunnels dug out of the soft sandy soil, and I come to this spot every year at this time to try to film and photograph them in among the pink sea thrift, and, hopefully, to film some rabbit kittens too.

Rabbits are by no means rare in the UK, with the population standing at around 36 million, but the species has undergone declines and fluctuations in recent years. Not native to the UK, it's thought that they were first introduced by the Romans, and over hundreds of years have become naturalized. They are now an integral part of the Great British Countryside. Their warrens supply refuges for other species and even ground-nesting birds such as puffins and Manx shearwaters, and even little owls, providing them ample places in which to raise their young. And the saying 'to breed like rabbits', meaning to reproduce prolifically, is indeed accurate. A female doe can give birth roughly every five to six weeks during the breeding season, which runs from January through to July or August, and each of her litters can have between three and seven kittens! A young rabbit is also able to reproduce at just four months old, so all of this has significantly contributed to their success as a species.

But despite how common they are, there is nothing more delightful than watching them jump around during the summer months in the evening sunlight with the ocean behind them. I often say that these rabbits are the poshest rabbits in the UK as they've made their home in the perfect location. They have the perfect sea view – one that a rich second-home-owner would pay millions for – but these rabbits get it for free! And this is why I have nicknamed them sea bunnies.

I get to my usual spot and set up my camera, and as I look at the swathes of green grass that merge into the rocky outcrops and eventually into the ocean below, I see my first few sets of pink ears darting around just beneath where I am, on a lower elevation. Rabbits can be very flighty when you're trying to film or photograph them. They're a food source for most passing predators, including stoats and weasels, buzzards and foxes, and even the peregrine that can be found along this coastal stretch. Lacking any fancy colouration like that of the six-spot burnet moth to dissuade predators, rabbits rely on their extremely quick reactions to avoid predation and will dart underground at even the slightest movement. So this means that, once I get into position, I point my camera straight at the multiple holes in among the pink sea thrift and just sit and wait. I have found this to be the best method, especially when trying to photograph the kittens, who are often less flighty than the adults and sometimes will come out of a hole and just sit there – almost as if they are posing!

I sit for about 40 minutes, watching and waiting as the sun gets lower. The sky turns into a magnificent mix of pinks and oranges with a tinge of purple, and swallows dart in the evening air catching insects before they head to roost. It is always a bit of a wait when I come here, as my presence in walking over and sitting down always makes them head to ground. But then I see a small movement, and a pair of tiny ears pop out of one of the holes in the dark green grass in among the pink sea thrift. I then glimpse the side of an eye and some long whiskers – it's a rabbit kitten!

As I wait in silence, this little ball of fluff appears from the hole and sits just on the edge of the entrance, sniffing the air, continuously alert. It definitely knows I'm here but it almost seems to be working out if I might be a threat, so I stay completely still and almost hold my breath. After a few minutes the little rabbit kitten is more at ease and begins to groom itself – which is tremendously endearing! I do some filming and then take some photographs, which I look through quickly on my viewfinder. I mean, you can't really go wrong with a rabbit kitten grooming itself in among the pink sea thrift at sunset. Every single angle and image is adorable! So after about an hour I decide to be on my way, and as soon as I move, the rabbit kitten's ears prick up and it darts back underground into the safety of the warren, just as I knew it would.

Every year, filming and photographing the rabbits is one of my wildlife highlights of the summer. Even though they are a species that we see all the time here in the UK, I think it is important to remind ourselves of the incredible wildlife we have at home and really remember just how lucky we are. This is a very special spot, one that I will continue to visit each summer to try to see the beautiful sea bunnies.

# AN UNEXPECTED ENCOUNTER

If there is one thing about wildlife, no matter how much research and preparation you put in, you can never be certain of what might happen or what you might stumble across when out in the field. You can put months of effort into tracking species, working out their movement patterns and behaviours, giving yourself the best possible chance to capture their beauty on film, but really, when it comes to being out in nature, we never know what might turn up. Wildlife doesn't read the script. But that is what makes it so exciting, and the more you are out there, the more unexpected encounters you will have.

It's early morning, 6.15am. I have just arrived at one of my favourite stretches of river and woodland. I'm not looking for any species in particular today so I have brought Isabelle with me for an amble through the woods. The forecast is warm and bright, so I've decided to make a day of it and just see what I can find. Isabelle is delighted when we step out of the car and she immediately gets the zoomies in the car park. She knows where we are. This is one of her favourite places in Cornwall, as well as mine, and a very popular site with families, dog walkers and holidaymakers. We start to make our way across the Respryn Bridge and into the woodland that runs adjacent to the River Fowey bubbling to our right.

Lanhydrock is one of the most beautiful places in Cornwall, and one I visit frequently. It's a site owned and managed by the National Trust just south of Bodmin and it is open to the public all year round. Many people come here to see the gardens, cycle the trails, and take a look at the old Victorian manor house. But, lovely as all that is, I always head straight down to the bottom of the estate to Respryn, as the woodlands alongside the River Fowey are filled with wildlife. Some sort of magical encounter happens nearly every time I visit. The semi-ancient woodlands support a whole host of species. Roe deer, badgers and foxes roam the woodland edges, and tawny owls sit on the branches of old oaks – if you're lucky you might catch a glimpse of one at first light on one of the trails. This is also the exact spot where I saw my first, and only, lesser spotted woodpecker, the rarest woodpecker we have in the UK.

Due to the estate's popularity, however, it does get extremely busy with groups and with families, so we always try to come at first light to beat the rush – because crowds are rarely good for wildlife spotting.

As we wander along the path at a slow pace, taking in the surroundings and soaking up the birdsong, I hear my first find of the morning: a loud and distinctive call, 'dwip-dwip, dwip-dwip', which it sings in repetitive phrases. I cast my eyes up to the canopy, scanning the surrounding tree trunks and branches as the call is getting louder so it must be close. Then I see a streak of pale blue dart behind the trunk of an old oak to the right of me. It must be round the other side, I say to myself, so I decide to try getting a little bit closer, and as I do it appears. One of the UK's most lovely woodland specialists, this species is famous for its ability to walk up and down tree trunks as it searches for its invertebrate prey, which it plucks from the tiny crevices in the bark during the spring and summer months. Right before me, I can see its wonderful blue back plumage and orange chest, its white head and black eye stripe. It is a striking nuthatch!

The population of nuthatch in these woods is very healthy, and on nearly every visit, even if I don't see one I always hear them. Nuthatches are known to be rather sedentary birds as they won't travel far from where they hatched, so if you do come across them in your area you can be pretty certain that you'll come across them again. During the spring and summer their diet will consist predominantly of small invertebrates, but during the autumn and winter they will switch to nuts and seeds, which they will cache in crevices in tree bark to see them through harder times. This is where they get their name.

I watch as it scuttles frantically up and down the trunk of the tree until it flutters off into the dense woodland. Even if I see nothing else today I would be happy going home just having seen a nuthatch, but little do I know what is in store just around the river bend. . .

Isabelle and I head down the trail and set up camp just on the corner where we usually sit. I take out her bowl, pour her some water and give her a treat so that she knows we will be here for a while. This corner has, over the years, delivered some incredible encounters – with dippers, with kingfishers and even with a family of mandarin ducks that decided to have their nest high up in one of the old oaks that towers over the river bend. So I'm hopeful that today this magical corner will deliver something special once again.

Hours and hours go by and nothing shows up. The time has disappeared and it's now around 3.30pm! All we have seen are some grey wagtails bobbing up and down on the rocky part of the riverbed that sticks out in front of us. They have been lovely to watch, with their handsome yellow, grey and white plumage, dipping away catching flying insects, but as far as Respryn goes, this has been a pretty bad turnout for wildlife.

I look at Isabelle and say, 'Should we go?' She has demolished all of her snacks, as well as mine, so I think it's about time we called it a day.

I start to take my camera off the tripod and look up directly in front of me above the water. I see what I think at first is a wren, but it's flying very strangely, although it is brown and around the same size. I do a double take and watch it for a few more seconds, completely perplexed as my brain goes into overdrive trying to identify what on earth this could be at 3.30pm in the afternoon in August. Is it a hummingbird hawk-moth? No, I think, it can't be.

I watch it as it flies above the surface of the water, circling up and down, then it heads straight to the water's surface and opens its mouth to take a drink. As it skims the surface of the river with its mouth wide open I see two tiny black eyes, a pink face and white sharp teeth. I can't believe my eyes. . . it's a bat!

Out of the 17 breeding bat species we have in the UK, all are strictly nocturnal and are very rarely seen out in the day. Being the only true flying mammal in the world, bats will hide away and sleep during daylight hours and will emerge at dusk when the light begins to fade. They hunt their insect prey using echolocation, and then, as dawn breaks, they will head back to their roosts. So this is a real shock, to say the least!

'Shit!' I say to myself, as I scramble to put my camera back on the tripod. Never in a million years did I think I would see a bat out in the daytime, and so close as well! As I stand up to get closer to the riverbank I slip and nearly fall in the water but hold my camera above my head, because, let's be honest, I don't care if I get wet and dirty but I do care if I ruin my camera. But due to my frenzied panic, Isabelle is now up and running around doing circles, the hairs standing up on her back all the way down to the tip of her tail. She has summoned her wolf DNA, and is alert and ready to protect her mummy at all costs. And now she seems to think that there's some sort of danger nearby due to me jumping up, clambering about, and swearing about six times in a matter of seconds. With the pair of us in an utter delirium of excitement and confusion, complete chaos has descended upon this usually picturesque and calming corner of the river bend!

The bat continues to swoop down to drink from the river, before flying back up into the air, circling around and drinking again. It must be thirsty, I think to myself, as I manage to lock my camera onto the tripod. In the last few months in Cornwall we have had severe drought, with only a light sprinkle of rain here and there. Everything is bone dry and has been now for weeks. Bats will only come out in the daytime for a couple of reasons: first, if they are disturbed, which is highly implausible given the location and the fact that there is no one else around; second, if they are sick; or third, if they are really hungry or thirsty. Given recent conditions, I can only assume that this poor bat is incredibly dehydrated and has come out very early to try to source some water as it keeps circling back round to drink more and more!

I put my camera into 4K at 120 frames per second and just hope for the best. I'm shaking too much to even attempt to take any photographs, so hopefully I'll at least get a bit of slow-mo footage that is half usable. As I watch it go back and forth I notice the size of the ears and think that it must be a brown long-eared bat – the ears are huge! This identification would also make sense given that they prefer to live in woodland and will roost in old trees. Although I'm aware that we have them here in Cornwall it's a species I never expected to see! I hardly take a breath as I just can't believe it!

Then, after a few minutes, it swoops off back into the dense woodland and a sense of calm washes over me. That really was a stress-filled few minutes after having been completely relaxed all day, and I sit back down on the ground. I look through my footage and there might be enough there to make something with, but not much, as even with stabilization in the edit you can clearly see how much I was shaking.

Nonetheless, what an incredible few moments it was. We head back to the car park and the main trail is now busy with afternoon ramblers, who all give me funny looks as I'm covered in mud after my escapade along the riverbank. But it was definitely worth it as this is a species I have never seen before and most likely will never see again. This is what I mean when I say the more time you spend out in nature the more amazing and once-in-a-lifetime wildlife experiences you will have. The unexpected encounters are the ones that you remember for the rest of your life.

# YOUNG ONES

The blustering wind soars past my face. It is strong. It is relentless. I feel my eyes start to tear up as the first salty drop streams down my cheek. This singular tear feels like an icy channel as the wind lashing me head-on is making what would be a warm trickle feel like a polar surge direct from the Atlantic.

But I am by no means upset – quite the contrary. These are the exact conditions to try to film a species found on the North Cornwall coast in abundance, and I'm heading to a spot that I know they frequent. It is this wind that will, hopefully, make my sightings even better as the weather is perfect for them. But whenever it's windy my eyes always well up, so though it looks like I'm crying, in fact I could not be more excited.

This evening I'm walking up past Fistral beach in Newquay and up towards Pentire headland. Known for its idyllic views overlooking Crantock on the left and Fistral to the right, swarms of people come here to watch the sunset, especially at this time of year. But, given the wind, I feel that this evening may be a quiet one.

I leave the tarmacked pavement and go up the stony path towards the coastal cliff edges and then head on to the headland itself, following the well-trodden grassy paths left by years of people walking these trails. I'm greeted by a few herring gulls soaring overhead and the tufty grass surrounding me is filled with bright yellow flowers dancing in the wind, tall bright green stems scattered with golden stars. When you look closer you can see that they are peppered with what look like long orange and black sweets, almost identical to perfectly round pick-and-mix strung together on tiny bits of thread and hung on the yellow flowers for decoration. But *these* pick-and-mix are certainly not sweets. In fact you should never put one of these 'sweets' in your mouth because, aside from tasting vile, they are also toxic.

At this time of year the ragwort is in full bloom and it grows in abundance around the headlands of the North Cornwall coast. Flowering from around June through to November, it is actually classified as a weed, but it's a very important plant species for a whole host of pollinators. It is one of the most visited wildflowers by butterflies and over 200 invertebrate species have been recorded using the plant. Ragwort is particularly vital for these orange and black pick-and-mix, which are actually cinnabar moth caterpillars, one of our cyanide moths. The caterpillars feed on the ragwort and can assimilate the toxins so that they become toxic themselves, their colouration and taste warding off any potential predators (much like the six-spot burnet moth we spoke about earlier). Cinnabar moth caterpillars are particularly ferocious and have cannibalistic tendencies: if the ragwort runs out they will turn on each other. (I have actually seen this before, a few years ago when filming them, and it is a pretty gruesome sight!)

I carry on around the corner to an area on the cliff ledge that is sheltered by some old stone walls and is filled with English stonecrop and the odd patch of sea campion. I sit down on the bouncy grass trying to avoid the thistles and look out over the open ocean to the Lewinnick Lodge, a very popular restaurant that is located on Pentire headland – a place where I have spent many a Friday evening. But not tonight.

I know that the species I'm hoping to film this evening nests along these cliffs somewhere. In previous years I have tried to locate the exact spot, but to no avail. The embankment gives way to the ocean not far from where I'm sitting and it is a sheer drop down, so I can only peek so far over the edge before it becomes dangerous. But this species will use the same nest site year on year if the area has sufficient resources. Well, I say nest site, but these birds don't really build a nest. Females lay between four and five eggs around April time and will use natural cavities in old trees and old buildings, and even use nest boxes.

Here on the Cornish coast a breeding pair will find a suitable and tucked-away crevice on the rocky outcrops in which to raise their young. Breeding pairs are largely monogamous and the male and female will separate after the breeding season, expanding their ranges and usually coming back together the following year. On average these birds live to around four years old, yet they have been recorded in the wild living up to fifteen years! So once you have a reliable nesting site you can be pretty sure you will have a good few years in which to photograph them.

This is better, I say to myself. I'm sitting against the stone wall and in a slight depression in the grass. I'm well sheltered from the wind. 'Cosy' might be pushing it but it's a lot better than the walk up.

After around ten minutes of waiting, I look up to my right and see an adult hovering. It is too far away to make out if it's a male, with handsome blue-grey head plumage, auburn back, black-tipped tail feathers and dappled white chest, or a female, which are more dappled and brown all over. It swoops down along the cliff edge and out of sight, using the prevailing wind to soar with ease, hardly even making a wing beat! Then in a matter of seconds it reappears right in front of me. Only a few feet away, it looks me straight in the eye before swooping away again, clearly as shocked to see me as I am to see it! A fabulous female kestrel!

One of the most successful birds of prey in the UK, kestrels can be found throughout rural areas, but also now in towns and cities, particularly in large parks and around wasteland areas. As long as there is an ample food supply (voles), you can be pretty sure that a kestrel won't be too far away. They are famous for their ability to hover in mid-air and they do this by flying into the prevailing wind at a matching speed, and, as they do so, they fan their tail feathers and extend their wing tips, which enables them to hover in the perfect position to look for prey below. Their eyesight is also impeccable and they can even spot prey items such as invertebrates from as far as 50m (164ft) away, and are also able to see in ultra-violet, which enables them to track the urine tails of voles in the long thick grass. All in all, they are top avian predators.

The female is now out of sight, but having seen her is an excellent sign. Given the time of year, her presence means that there must be fledglings here somewhere. So I decide to get up out of my grassy nook and venture a little closer to the cliff edge – just far enough so that I have more of a view of the rugged cliff faces below. I scan them closely, squinting in the wind. One thing about kestrels is that they become perfectly camouflaged against the brown-grey rocks. They can often be right in front of you resting on a rocky outcrop and you won't even notice them until they take flight.

But then I spot them: not one, but two! They don't have their full adult plumage yet and are more brown and dappled in colouration, and they're smaller than the adult female. They are perched together looking around at their surroundings: two kestrel fledglings!

Once kestrel chicks have hatched, they won't be ready to fledge for around a month and will be provisioned by both parents. Like all raptor species kestrel chicks are altricial, but are born with quite well developed downy white feathers. After a few weeks they will lose their white down and begin to form their adult plumage. Quite often on *Springwatch* we will have a kestrel nest as one of our live wildlife cameras, and when the chicks are at that in-between stage between fluffy down and adult plumage they really aren't at their most attractive! But I love going into the camera truck every morning to see how they are doing, and the process of them losing their down seems to happen so quickly. The chicks will semi-fledge at around four weeks old but won't venture too far, and will stay in the parents' territory for a further month or so. This is when the parents teach them how to hunt and survive before they head off on their own.

I set my camera up facing the prevailing wind, with the two kestrel fledglings perched on the rock. They are far away, and it is quite dark now that it's 7pm and overcast, but what an amazing shot this would be – two kestrel fledglings perched together! As I get into position, however, one of the fledglings takes off, flying not far but just out of sight. The other one is still on the rock so I take about a hundred photographs, as my camera shakes in the wind, hoping to perhaps get at least one that is OK.

I quickly scan through my photos and definitely have enough, but I stay for a further half an hour before deciding to call it an evening and head home. I did hope that the second young kestrel would come back and perch, but being able to photograph just one young one was still fantastic!

I leave the headland, with the kestrel fledgling still on its rock and the wind still relentless. I had hoped to get one of the fledglings in flight, but I'm very happy to have got some shots regardless. And I hope that this breeding pair of adults continue to have successful broods right on my doorstep year after year so that I can have some more incredible encounters with their young ones.

A fulmar adult with
a young chick

The ghost-like grey heron
at Porth Reservoir

The nation's favourite bird: an inquisitive
robin perched on a branch

A linnet in winter looking for
seed-bearing plants for survival

A juvenile kestrel on Pentire
headland in Newquay

Masters of their environment: a kingfisher perfectly still
before diving into the water at lightning speed

Jam faces: a male goldfinch with its red facial patch and tweezer-like beak

A mouse in the garage

A long-tailed tit in spring in among the blackthorn blossom

A rabbit captured on the DSLR camera trap

Isabelle: my white German shepherd with me on the Cornish coast

First encounters: a fox cub resting in the magical evening light

A summer visitor: the swallow comes to the UK in breeding season

A pod of dolphins with bubbles rising to the water's surface

A Cornwall beaver out on land, feeding

A staring competition: the inquisitive roe deer buck
can stay very still and stare for minutes on end

The ecosystem engineers: one of the beavers that was introduced
to the wild enclosure at the Cornwall Beaver Project

# September

# LANUGO WATCH

September. The dawn of a new season is just around the corner and there is somehow a marked shift in the natural world around us. The days get slightly shorter, and the hedgerows start to show off the first fruits of their early autumnal bounty. Filled with blackberries, rosehips, sloes, elderberries and hawthorn, it's almost as if they are extending an invitation for the winter migrant birds that will be gracing our shores once more in just a few short weeks. All around the air is filled with white fluffy seed heads that look like fairies dancing on the breeze. These are mostly thistle seeds, among others at this time of year, but I have always called them fairies as they usually appear in the middle of August and are in abundance when September begins. My birthday is on 1 September, and when I was young, I thought that these seed heads were actual fairies who would start to appear just in time for my birthday celebrations. And, to be honest, I still like to think this now.

But although we're aware of the wonderful sights, smells and sounds of September, we don't often associate this month with new life. Here in Cornwall, however, as the start of the pupping season for one of the UK's most iconic marine mammals, this is exactly what happens at this time of year.

This evening wasn't meant to be a wildlife night. I had just returned from a week-long shoot and, apart from being exhausted, I had a sizeable pile of washing to deal with. But at around 5.30pm my mate Dave rang, saying that he had to go on duty and inviting me to join him. This was an unusual sort of duty: to guard a baby mammal that had been separated from its mother and needs to be watched by volunteers from dawn until dusk to ensure that the public or dogs don't disturb it. The washing can wait and I can sleep later, I thought to myself. Within five minutes I was ready and out the door, camera in hand.

If you visit the Cornish coast at any time of the year you can be pretty sure that you'll see one of these species. We have a good population of them here, and they're often seen bobbing out on the open ocean or hauled out on a rock or beach. In fact, in the UK, around the country's coastline, we are responsible for roughly 40 per cent of the global population, making it incredibly important that we look after them. Yet today there are more red squirrels than this species, and more African elephants, which is a sobering thought. They have highly tuned senses – sight, hearing and smell – so if you can see them, they can see you. Given the level of tourism in Cornwall, disturbance is a huge issue. This is why British Divers Marine Life Rescue (BDMLR), marine mammal medics like my friend Dave, are now coming into their busiest time of the year. It is grey seal pupping season.

We drive out past Bedruthan Steps and down to Porth Mear cove, an idyllic and extraordinarily picturesque part of the coastline, and one that is quite tucked away. Joined by our friend Steph, we walk down to the beach area where the other marine mammal medics have been, passing them on the way. They have just finished their shift watching a tiny grey seal pup that had somehow been separated from its mother and had ended up on the beach.

Grey seal pupping season happens at different times around the UK, but will usually start in September and run through to around January or February. Cornwall is the first place in the UK to get pups – now as early as August! – and pupping starts just a little bit later as you move clockwise around the coastline. It takes place around September or October in Wales; then November in Scotland; and from around the end of November through to December on the east coast and Norfolk.

The first two or three weeks of a grey seal pup's life are quite possibly their most important. When first born they weigh around 13kg (26lb 10oz) to 14kg (30lb 11oz), but will triple their body weight in just a three-week period as their mother's milk is roughly 50–60 per cent fat, on average gaining 2kg (4lb 7oz) per day. The pups suckle from their mothers for around ten minutes between five and six times each day, and this allows them to develop a decent layer of blubber so they can survive on their own in the wild.

During these first few weeks the pups won't go into the water and are covered in a white fluffy coat, or lanugo. But once their lanugo begins to moult and they weigh between 40kg (88lb 30oz) and 50kg (110lb 4oz), their mother will leave them to fend for themselves, and they will survive off their fat reserves built up from her milk while they learn how to hunt.

Mothers will congregate on pupping beaches, sites that will be used by grey seals for generation after generation. It is on these beaches that they give birth, but also mate with dominant bull males once the pups are weaned. The females (called cows) become fertile quite quickly after weaning their pups, but because of delayed implantation (the process described earlier in relation to badgers), they won't become pregnant until the following year, and will nearly always return to the same beach to give birth.

Porth Mear cove, however, is quite a distance from one of the well-used pupping beaches on this stretch of the coast. Perhaps the mother did indeed give birth here. Or, if the pup was born elsewhere, it is possible, given recent rough conditions, that it was washed away from its mother at high tide and ended up here. Whatever the explanation, at this stage in its life, and given how exposed it is, the pup could end up in serious trouble.

We sit down on the grassy verge that is far back from the beach itself, as we want to keep a watchful eye but not disturb the pup. And as we look out to the water we can see the mother bobbing around, which is a good sign. But the other medics told us that she had only come to shore once to feed the pup during the day, which certainly isn't enough for a small fluffy white coat!

Around 15 minutes go by, and we haven't had any views of the pup. We were told that it was lying down, hidden out of view behind a rocky outcrop on the beach, only to be seen if it pops its head up. You would think that the white coat would make them stand out, but, against the mixture of rocks, sand, washed-up debris and seaweeds, they are actually perfectly camouflaged!

While we are on duty, a few people go by and one family tries to walk on the beach. But Dave explains the situation – that we are trying to ensure that no one goes onto the beach as it may stop the mum from coming to shore to let the pup feed. The family are completely fine, as is a man on a dog walk, but one couple are very much not. As Dave explains what we are doing this couple get really angry. 'We live here, you can't tell us we can't go on a beach, how dare you!' Dave spends a good ten minutes repeatedly and calmly going over the situation. Eventually they leave, but there really was no need for the way they acted. Unfortunately, this happens a lot – and more often than you'd think.

All the seal organizations and charities in Cornwall work incredibly hard trying to protect our seal population. What's even better is that they all work together for the same cause –

to ensure that our grey seals are thriving and surviving. The Cornish Seal Sanctuary (for whom I'm an ambassador), BDMLR and the Cornwall Seal Group Research Trust are all fantastic at what they do. They work round the clock, particularly in pupping season, and they deserve more recognition for the work that they do. It really shouldn't be tricky for them – especially when it comes to the public and disturbance.

The light is starting to fade now, and we won't stay long past dark as we won't be able to see. Hopefully, no one will be walking on the beach at night in any case. But all of a sudden we see a tiny white head pop up from behind the rock, with its long black whiskers and jet black eyes. The little white coat has decided to start moving!

When you see them first-hand you can see exactly why people would want to get close to them. They are quite possibly one of the most adorable pups we have in the UK! And of course, many people aren't aware of the risks for the young pups of human disturbance. I remember when I was at the Cornish Seal Sanctuary and one of the workers said that a seal pup had been abandoned because a couple had put their two-year-old child on it in order to take photographs, making it look as if the child was riding the pup. I mean, there's not understanding the delicate issue of disturbance and then there's outright ignorance and awful behaviour. This story still makes me shudder.

You should, of course, never, ever approach a seal pup or touch it, as even your smell could make the mother abandon it. The best thing to do if you spot a white coat on its own is to call your local seal rescue, then they can come out and assess the situation to decide if the pup needs assistance. This is exactly what happened in our case, and why we are now on duty at Porth Mear cove.

We watch on as this tiny creature decides to start wriggling its way down the beach towards the shoreline. They are funny on land as they move along rather awkwardly on their tummies. They are definitely more graceful in the water! Along the way, as it gets closer to the sea, it lets out little calls. These animals are very vocal, and it's said that in the past sailors approaching the shore could hear their calls and thought they were ghosts or mythical creatures – but these haunting sounds we now know to be those of the grey seal. These vocalizations are not only an important form of communication, but a mother can recognize her pup even in busy breeding colonies just from its call and its smell.

'Poor thing, it must be hungry,' I turn and say to Dave, as we watch it look out to sea, as if it knows its mother is there bobbing around somewhere. And lo and behold, around four minutes later she appears – a beautiful female with her long roman nose and sleek grey-blue dappled skin. She drags herself onto the beach and greets her baby with a few nose touches, whisker snuffles and sniffs, then she rolls onto her side and the pup begins to feed. I do sometimes wonder what it must be like to have the whiskers of a grey seal. Being more sensitive than our fingertips, a seal's whiskers enable them to catch their fish prey underwater as well as sense their environment and communicate with other seals. Even grey seals that have gone blind have been found living in the wild, thanks to their whiskers!

The light has almost gone so it is too dark to take any photographs, but we sit for another five minutes and watch before we decide to leave, very carefully and quietly. The pup is still suckling when we go.

You will be pleased to know that, after continued monitoring from BDMLR marine mammal medics, this pup made it, moulting and putting on enough weight to eventually make it out to sea.

The mother continued to feed it, thanks to the work of the volunteers ensuring that disturbance was kept to a minimum for the following three weeks. They really do dedicate themselves to the seals here in Cornwall, especially in pupping season. And long may their incredibly important work continue, so that we can watch more grey seal pups with their white fluffy lanugos for many years to come.

# MIGRATION STOPOVER

One thing about living on the Cornish coast, the most southerly part of the UK, is that we do get some rather unusual vagrant birds appearing on our shores. Each spring we get a flurry of hoopoes that overshoot on their migration from Africa to Europe, having been blown off course, and this always brings in the birdwatching crowd. I remember there was almost an ornithological festival when a European roller turned up a couple of years ago near the village of Praze-an-Beeble. When a brown booby bird appeared off the coast of St Ives (the first ever recorded on British shores) the entire UK birdwatching community went into full twitcher meltdown. And when I say meltdown, I mean meltdown.

But there is one bird that we now see each spring and autumn along its migration route here in Cornwall thanks to its having been a bit of a conservation success story, and we are seeing it more and more frequently along our waterways year on year. It's an incredible raptor species that became extinct in England as a breeding bird in 1840, due to relentless persecution. They were shot by landowners as it was thought they threatened fish stocks, and their eggs were also highly valued by egg collectors. But their beautiful plumage and stature were also prized by taxidermists, and wealthy people wanted them stuffed in their homes. In more recent years, through stringent conservation efforts coupled with continued and diligent legal protection, these undeniably astonishing birds are, thankfully, on the up across the UK, with estimates stating that we now have around 1,500 individuals!

The last few weeks for me have been incredibly busy and I have hardly been at home. Filming a new series for BBC Earth, I have been all over the place, only returning for a few days here and there before heading back out on the road. But when I arrive home I find out that one of these birds has been on the Gannel estuary next to my house for the last two weeks! This in itself is quite a long time for an individual to stop off at the same place – so it could have been one of this year's fledglings. Perhaps it is a young one taking advantage of the excellent fish stock that the estuary provides while plucking up the courage to start its incredibly long migration to Africa, making the 3,100-mile journey for the first time.

Isabelle and I walk down to the Gannel at high tide, as this is when the bird had been seen hunting across the water. We walk down one of the paths under some huge conifer trees alongside the estuary, and I set my camera up on rocks pointing directly towards the treeline running adjacent to Penpol Creek. But while we're there a man in a kayak gently paddles past us and says, without a care in the world, 'Take it you're looking for the osprey? It left this morning. . .' and paddles on his way.

Needless to say, I am more than disappointed. Having an osprey quite literally on my doorstep is a rarity in itself! And to then have missed it was actually quite devastating. They are magnificent birds and I have only ever had the privilege of seeing one once before when we were based in the Cairngorms in Scotland for *Springwatch*. It was an evening when we didn't have a live show and a group of us were driving to get pizza (as we like to do during a live TV run!). My old producer (and all-round legendary superstar) Laura Howard shouted at the top of her lungs while in the car 'Osprey!' We looked out to our left and there it was – flying above a loch, its white and brown dappled plumage standing out among the conifers. Its sheer size took your breath away. It was at Loch Garten in the Cairngorms where the first pair of ospreys attempted to breed in the UK once again in the 1950s. Birds had started to return to the area a few years earlier on their migration route from Africa to Scandinavia, and when the first pair attempted to breed, the fantastic RSPB set up 'Operation Osprey', keeping the birds under surveillance and monitoring them 24 hours a day! The first year of breeding the nest failed, but since then, ospreys have successfully bred there year after year. The RSPB's work in protecting these birds has significantly contributed to their recolonization. Loch Garten is still to this day one of the best places to see these birds during the summer months.

But there is another spot, here in Cornwall on the south coast, where I know they can often be seen at this time of year. Now that I have the osprey bug, I decide to head there the very next day.

Devoran Quay is located just above Falmouth and is an old port that was used for exporting ore from the local Cornish mines and importing wood and timber, mostly between Cornwall and South Wales. It is part of Restronguet Creek, a tributary of Carrick Roads, which leads into one of the estuaries of the River Fal. Now that all industry has ceased, it is a very picturesque and popular spot for boat owners and holidaymakers, particularly during the summer, and, being tidal, the mudflats are excellent for a host of wading birds. The woods running adjacent to the water's edge support a myriad of species. It really is a fantastic spot to visit on a sunny afternoon in search of wildlife!

My friend Dave and I pull up in one of the lay-bys next to the creek and spot a couple of people on the shoreline, one with a long lens on a monopod and the other with a birding scope. 'That's a good sign,' I say to Dave as we pick up our camera bags and step out of the car. The tide is high and it is a beautiful warm day, with the crisp feeling of autumn in the air.

Each and every year ospreys are known to stop at the quay on their way back to Africa. Some stay only for a few days, but others will stay longer. I had checked the Cornwall Bird Sightings website run by Cornwall Bird Watching Preservation Society (CBWPS) the evening before and for the last few days an osprey has been seen here. So Dave and I are hopeful that we haven't missed it like the one that's already left in Newquay.

As a species, ospreys are the second most widely distributed raptor in the world after the peregrine falcon, and, apart from Antarctica, they can be found on every continent. They are a superb bird of prey that has evolved for a life out on open water and their ability to hunt for prey in both salt and fresh water has contributed to their success around the globe. Watching them hunt with that impressive wingspan of around 1.5m (4¾ft) is extraordinary. They dive into a stoop at speeds of up to 77 miles per hour from distances of up to 40m (131ft) in order to catch their fish. This is something that I think every wildlife lover should try to see at least once in their lifetime. It is more than impressive!

They are built unlike any other bird of prey. As they dive down to the water's edge, they will completely submerge themselves in the water – often to depths of 1m (3¼ft). They hit the water talons out first, and streamline their powerful wings behind their backs. Their nostrils have the ability to close upon entering the water and they also have a nictitating membrane, so they can see in the murky depths. They have four-toed feet that are covered in spiny pads underneath, which helps them grasp the wet fish. Their outer toe is reversible, and they use it to manipulate the placement of the fish between their talons so that their dinner can't wriggle away, but this repositioning can also minimize drag when pulling the fish out of the water and in flight. The osprey has to be one of the most breathtaking birds of prey that we have in the UK, and the fact that we are able to catch a glimpse of them here in Cornwall is magic!

We stand at the edge of the quay, having a bit of a chat with the fellow birdwatchers. One of them tells us that he has been coming here every day at high tide for the last four days and that the osprey has been appearing from the woods on the far side and then flying into the middle of the body of water and using one of the boat masts as its lookout. So, we stand and wait.

'It's on the move!' shouts the other man who hasn't once taken his eye away from his bird-scope. 'Along the treeline, headed straight for the middle!' I switch my camera on, locked on the tripod head and ready to go, and scan across the water's edge, but I can only see a few black-backed gulls in the sky.

'I can't see it! Where?' I say with a tinge of excited frustration and anticipation in my voice.

'Look up, on top of the boat mast!' the other man says.

I scan up and into the middle of the creek, and way in the distance I see a raptor figure sitting right on the top of the tallest boat mast. It really is incredibly far away, so I look through my viewfinder, and then I see it. That brown and white dappled plumage with a slender sharp pointed black beak and piercing yellow eyes. It's an osprey! And my first ever here in Cornwall!

Given its size, I think it's possibly a female. Females are known to be around 20 per cent larger than males, and this one is huge! It also appears to have a substantial patch of brown on the chest, another sign that it could be female, although this feature can be a tricky one to rely on. But the best way to sex an osprey is to have a male and female next to one another, something you only really see when monogamous breeding pairs return to their nesting sites.

This bird is definitely too far away to take any photographs, but, between us, I'm not fussed in the slightest – just to see one is spectacular enough!

As Dave and I, along with our two new bird friends, watch on, the osprey starts to fidget on the boat mast. Then, in the blink of an eye, it spreads its wings and takes to flight! I quickly put my eye to my viewfinder and follow it with my lens. Unfortunately, it has decided to head back towards the treeline to hunt, which is too far away for human eyes to make out, and any footage or photographs I take would be unusable. So, for this moment, I decide not to even attempt to take any shots and instead watch the action through my long lens (which I also use as binoculars, as it saves carrying something else!).

We watch the osprey dive down to the water, but then emerge quickly afterwards. 'Did she get anything?' I ask the group, to which the man with the scope replies, 'No, not this time.'

Ospreys might be incredible hunters, but it is said that, on average, out of every four to five hunting attempts only one will be successful. And now we watch as this bird gracefully flies down the creek towards the River Fal until it is out of sight.

Today wasn't my day for film or photography, but it was special all the same. To be able to see one of the most awe-inspiring and impressive birds of prey in the world on my doorstep is nothing short of extraordinary. A species that was absent here for so many years is now once again beginning to thrive at certain locations. This is always one of the best feelings for any wildlife lover: to know that a species is on the up! Ospreys in the UK still aren't quite out of the woods in terms of them thriving along all of our waterways, but they are off to a great start! And I really do hope that their population numbers here continue to rise, and then hopefully, one day, I will get my shot of one of these magnificent birds making its migration stopover.

# BUBBLES AND WHISTLES

It's 8.30am and I gaze out across the large blue expanse of the North Atlantic. Staring out to the ocean is known to be good for us. Shifting our brain into an almost-meditative state and changing its frequency is proven to make us feel less stressed, more tranquil and at peace. I watch the open ocean in front of me as it shimmers and twinkles in the morning sunlight, with the calming sound of the waves crashing on the shoreline and the calls of gulls filling the sky above. I couldn't feel more relaxed. There isn't a single ounce of breeze as sea salt lingers in the air and I watch a hummingbird hawk-moth feed on some honeysuckle in the hedgerow next to me, its wingbeats invisible to the naked eye and its fluffy body surrounded by a misty blurry haze. They have to be one of the most striking and exotic-looking day-flying moths in the UK, and can be seen from around June through to September. It's a migratory species that graces our shores after migrating north from southern Europe each year, and in 2022 we had an extraordinarily good year for them, with their numbers increasing ten-fold!

A hummingbird hawk-moth is a delight to see in itself, but on this warm bright September morning I'm not here to find wildlife goodies along the hedgerows. I'm heading out on the open ocean to find one of Cornwall's marine mammal specialities. . .

'Morning team! How are we all?' I shout down the street in the harbour, which, despite being early on a Tuesday morning in September, is full of the hustle and bustle of midsummer. This place in particular has to be one of the most popular spots with tourists throughout the year, a quintessential small coastal town that attracts people from all over the world due to its picturesque location on the North Cornwall coast and its world-class restaurants. It has even attracted quite the selection of celebrities over the years. Gordon Ramsay's house is just across the water in Rock, and locals have another name for the town, 'Padstein', coined for the other famous TV chef, Rick Stein, who has a selection of establishments in the vicinity.

I am, of course, in Padstow. But I'm not here for the fine dining or celebrity chefs, I'm here for the real stars of this area. . .

'Hello lovely, how've you been? Beautiful day for it!' says Jenny Simpson, one of the wildlife guides, in her soft Scottish tones. This morning I'm heading out on a Padstow Sealife Safari, one of my favourite wildlife trips in the whole county. I remember my first trip with them, with one of my best friends, and an incredible nature writer, Sophie Pavelle. I think we spent the entire two-hour trip screaming in sheer delight. Every time, you see something incredible out at sea, and the Sealife Safari team are among the best people in Cornwall – their knowledge of marine life in the area is outstanding. Should you visit Padstow I highly recommend booking a boat tour with them. I love them so much that they are even part of my itinerary on my own week-long Cornwall Wildlife Safari! Over the years they have had regular sightings of puffins, gannets, razorbills, guillemots, Manx shearwaters, sunfish, bottlenose and common dolphins, harbour porpoise, grey seals, and even some rarer sightings, though ones that are becoming more frequent around the Cornish coast, including minke whales, sei whales and even humpback! Of course, you never know what could pop up when you're out on a boat with them, and a lot of species are seasonal, but it's the not knowing and the anticipation that makes it a thrilling experience, always!

After having a bit of a gossip we make our way down the harbour steps and onto one of their RIB boats docked at the side of the quay. I decide to sit up front today, as in my experience I always get soaked sitting in the back – every single time. And today, given the still, calm and pretty much perfect conditions, I really want to try to take as many photographs as possible. I have my life jacket on and am sitting securely as the RIB starts to move and we head out of Padstow harbour.

As we pick up speed coming out of the bay, we travel past the Rumps and spot a large bull grey seal bottling in the water. Bottling is the term used for when seals stay completely still vertically in the water with just their heads poking out to breathe, an indication that they are resting. Even though you can only see the front of the seal's face, you can tell it's a male because of the broadness of the head. And as we head further out around Mouls island I can see shags, black-backed gulls and a few oystercatchers on the rocks below. A single northern gannet is bobbing around on the water, so I decide to take some shots quickly then put my camera away to protect it from sea spray before we head further up the coast.

Then, way out in the distance, up the coast past Port Isaac towards Tintagel, I spot them: what looks like a pair of tiny fins jumping in and out of the water, but easily recognizable in today's glass-like ocean. 'Over there!' I shout like an excited six-year-old, 'Dolphins!'

We are very lucky here in Cornwall to be able to see a few different species of dolphin around the coastline. Common and bottlenose are the most frequently sighted, but we also get Risso's, striped and Atlantic white-sided. Their intuitive and playful nature makes them a much-loved marine mammal not just in the UK, but around the world. Known for their intelligence and their social nature, they live in large groups called pods and this is an integral part of their lives. They have evolved to live this way as a form of protection, but they also communicate constantly with one another, hunt together and play together.

Intelligence is one of those things that is difficult to measure in animals other than ourselves without imposing our ingrained human beliefs and assumptions onto another species. In other words, it is difficult to assess the intelligence of a non-human animal without a hefty dose of anthropomorphism. That said, years of scientific research have enabled us to make inferences as to how intelligent dolphins are. And what the science shows is that they are pretty smart.

The complexity of their communication is one indication of this. They do not have vocal cords but communicate in a variety of whistles, trills, squeaks and burst-like chirps. These sounds also vary between different pods, suggesting that each pod of dolphins has its own dialect. It is also thought that they can identify one another by a 'signature whistle' and it is plausible to think that they may have a sense of 'self'. The ability to recognize oneself in a mirror is something that has only been attributed to species with higher levels of intelligence and has been found in elephants, orangutans, chimpanzees, manta rays, killer whales, Eurasian magpies and bottlenose dolphins. Moreover, dolphins have been found to recognize themselves in a mirror at merely seven months old, whereas a human child does so at around twelve months. Parental care is also long, and dolphin calves stay with their mothers for anywhere between three and six years, during which time the mother teaches all the life skills they need. It has also been found that dolphins can utilize tools, use echolocation to hunt and navigate through the water even under the cover of darkness, and will even eavesdrop on other dolphins' conversations.

As the RIB picks up speed it's almost as if we are flying towards them. I hold onto the hood of my jacket as my hair lashes my face and screw up my eyes, not wanting to lose sight of their dorsal fins. Then as we approach, we begin to slow down. I frantically pick up my bag and pull out my camera, and as I do Jenny shouts, 'Right in front towards the left-hand side!'

I look out and, lo and behold, a common dolphin is leaping in and out of the water. I swing my camera up and with the highest shutter speed that the light will allow, I hold my finger down and follow it, hoping to get at least one leap. Then the leaping disappears and Jenny shouts again: 'They're coming towards us, keep your eyes on the sides of the RIB.'

I want to look through my photos quickly to see if I've managed to actually get a shot of the dolphin leaping out of the water (the shot of all shots and one I have never managed to get), but there is no time. In what feels like a matter of seconds, the RIB is surrounded! An entire pod of common dolphins has come to play!

As I look to the side of the RIB I can count at least eight common dolphins! Their dark grey fins glimmer and shine in the morning sunlight as the water slides off them, their whitish flanks appearing as they emerge from the calm bobbing waves. There are even more on the other side! Dolphin pods on average can range from anywhere between three and thirty individuals, but superpods of hundreds and sometimes thousands exist. There aren't hundreds of dolphins around us right now, but there are certainly more than 15!

They are so close that if I held out my arm I could touch them with my fingers! And my long lens now is just too close. Jenny begins to reel off her facts about common dolphins for the group (and she is very, very good at it), but then something extraordinary happens: we hear them! We can actually hear their clicking and whistling: they are talking to one another!

In all of my years of coming on these boat trips I have never been so fortunate as to actually hear the dolphins communicate. Every time they emerge you can clearly hear their trills, whistles and clicks! Of course, we have lucked out with the weather conditions today as there isn't a single drop of wind, but to hear them communicating like this is something very, very special!

The pod stays with us for a good ten minutes, playing at the front of the RIB and swimming back and forth underneath it, then they begin to head up the coast. They have been too close for me to take any photos, but as they start moving slightly further away I try to take as many as possible before Jenny says, 'Right gang, let's leave them to it and start to make our way back.'

The dolphin pods along this stretch of the coast are very used to visitors on boats, but the team at Padstow Sealife Safaris keep wildlife ethics at the centre of what they do. Despite taking people out most days during spring and summer to try to spot dolphins, the team ensure that they never outstay their welcome, never, in a million years, chase the dolphins, and always allow the pods to come naturally towards the boat. They will get into the best position to see if the dolphins will come over to the boat of their own accord – but sometimes they don't, which is fine. We are just visitors to their world, out on the open ocean. It's as if the dolphins know they are rock stars with fans who want to get their shots, but, when it's time to leave, it's time to leave. This is why I call them the real stars of the area – because they are.

As we travel back down the coast, across the bay and into dock, I can't believe what we have just witnessed – to hear them like that and so close has to be one of my top wildlife experiences in the UK. I say goodbye to Jenny and the team and then sit on a bench to look through my photographs (which I have been busting to look at the whole time!). And I did manage to get a shot when that first dolphin was leaping out of the water. Is it blurry? Yes. Is it too far away? Yes. Is it the shot of all shots? Absolutely not. But I got one all the same! As I flick through, however, I realize that when the dolphins were close to the boat I did manage to get some really great shots of them coming in and out of the water with perfect bubble formations coming out of their blow holes! Which I'm very pleased with!

It has been a fantastic morning out on the ocean with Padstow Sealife Safaris, but then it always is. I'm already thinking about when I have time to come out again! To get so close to the dolphins that I could hear them talking to one another is something I will never, ever forget. And I can't wait to come out again soon, hopefully to photograph some more bubbles and hear some more whistles.

# October

# BRIGHT RED BEAKS

October. A time where autumn's majesty has fully graced us with her presence. The changing of bright green leaves to fiery orange, deep red or vibrant yellow presents us with a noticeable shift across the great British countryside, a shift that seems to happen right before our eyes. Fairy rings scatter open fields and we begin to see old fallen trees and forest floors come alive, peppered with the striking shapes and colours that autumn fungi bring. Reds, purples, oranges and whites can be seen throughout our woodlands, as if autumn's paintbrush has delicately taken to the landscape, using the natural world as a blank canvas to create a new and almost ethereal picture. The arrival of shorter days and longer nights has us rummage through our wardrobes to pull out jumpers, hats, gloves and scarfs, as our wildlife walks are now just a tad chillier. It really is a magical time of the year.

The symphony of our skies and hedgerows has now also changed. I have always said that it's the sound of birdsong that really makes us notice the change in the seasons, and if you spend a lot of time out in nature you will know what I mean. All of our hirundine species are now well on their migration route back to Africa, along with our warblers; the skylark is no longer singing; and as for the cuckoo, it is a distant memory.

But the bird I'm hoping to photograph this evening is one that can, thankfully, now be seen in Cornwall all year round. It's a species that is almost synonymous with the county, and is steeped in its history and culture – so much so that it is even on the Cornish coat of arms. Yet our coastal cliffs went quiet for 28 years when it became locally extinct in 1973, with the last breeding pair living on the cliffs around Newquay where I live today. But in 2001 something extraordinary happened: it returned naturally. And now it is here to stay.

I walk across Porth beach with my camera bag on my back. The tourists have now gone, and what would have been a bustling spot full of windbreaks, barbecues and screaming children just a few weeks ago is now nearly completely empty. I'm accompanied by just two lone dog walkers. Although the evening is warm, some mizzle has set in. I look further down the coast and see that the white fog has settled in between the headlands, moving slowly and ghostlike around the rugged cliffs. The sun is casting an orange hue and beaming rays on the parts of the coast that the mist hasn't reached. It is a very typical North Cornwall autumnal sky, and is like something out of a movie!

I walk off the beach and onto the pavement, heading straight uphill to Porth Island. A headland in Newquay laden with history, it was known as an Iron Age fort and still has remnants of Bronze Age ramparts and barrows. Due to its prominent height and views up and down the coast it was an important part of the coastline, and the beach itself was once used as a port for the village of St Columb Minor before the town of Newquay even existed. Now, however, it is one of the most popular spots in the areas surrounding Newquay and is filled with tourists during the spring and summer months getting their selfies up on the headland, with the sunset background perfect for Instagram. It is also a hotspot for wildlife, and I come here a lot to film rabbits, black-backed gulls, wheatears, gannets, oystercatchers and the occasional fulmar.

I have heard reports that the bird I'm after has now been spotted frequently on the island. And not just one of them, but two! They have been seen using their long beaks to probe the soft sandy soil for invertebrates such as beetles, leatherjackets (the larvae of crane flies), ants and small spiders. And it was a change in the prey abundance of invertebrate species around the cliff edges that is thought to have played a major role in their earlier demise along the Cornish coast. Apart from having to face the issue of hunting for taxidermy thanks to their incredible appearance, these birds were also seen as pests and were shot by farmers or threatened by egg collectors. But it was the change in farming practices that is thought to have had the biggest effect on their numbers. The increased use of pesticides, wiping out the target insects along with every other invertebrate, meant they had less to eat. Couple this with the removal of livestock grazing up to the cliff edges (moved further inland in a bid to make farm workers' jobs easier), and the result is that these birds pretty much disappeared. But now, thanks to landowners, farmers, conservation groups and scientists all working together, areas of coastal habitat are being managed suitably, creating swathes of short grassland filled with invertebrate life, which is perfect for them!

I head up over the first brow of the hill, with the mist settling to my right. Then I hear one: that famous and incredibly distinctive call that, once you've heard it, you will never misidentify. It's definitely a corvid of some sort, but it sounds more like a high-pitched 'chee-ow', often in repetitive phrases that seem to echo all around you. I look directly above me and see it, a black silhouette with characteristic prominent wing tips that look a bit like finger feathers, that bright curved crimson-red beak and crimson-red legs. It's a Cornish chough!

It's one of the smallest members of the crow family here in the UK, with a wingspan of between 70cm (27½in) and 90cm (35½in), and they are still one of the rarest to see. Numbers have been on the up in recent years, but because their populations are scattered and highly isolated around the west coast spanning Cornwall, Wales, the Isle of Man, Scotland and some coastal areas in Ireland, they remain a species that requires conservation monitoring as genetic viability is a cause for concern. The choughs that returned naturally to the Cornish coast were part of the Irish population, however, which is a good sign and shows that there is movement between these isolated groups, and this natural movement will, hopefully, bolster the overall health of choughs in the UK in the long run. This pioneering pair (as I like to call them) returned to our south coast and set up home on the Lizard Peninsula. They first bred successfully in 2002, which was the first time in 50 years that wild choughs had laid and raised young in the county! The dynamic duo went on to raise a whopping 44 fledglings that naturally started to move their way around the coastline. Now choughs can be seen all around the Cornish coast, particularly on more rugged and remote parts of the coast path. And 2023 was a huge success for them as we had a total of 39 breeding pairs that successfully fledged 112 youngsters!

The chough lands on the grass just out of view behind one of the old mounds, so I drop to the ground taking my camera out of my bag. The mizzle is now engulfing all of Porth Island, which is certainly not great for filming or photography, but hey ho, here we are. As I lock my camera onto the tripod head, I hear another bird above me and watch it swoop down and land behind the mound to join its fellow. That is one thing about choughs. If you see or hear one you can be certain that there are more around as they always move together. Breeding pairs are highly monogamous and will stay together all through the year. They will also use the same nest site year on year. Both the male and the female will build the nest using old twigs and grasses, often lining them with sheep's wool. The nest will be built in some sort of craggy crevice along the coastal headlands, though they have also been known to use old farm buildings, mine shafts and the old mining buildings at Botallack (one of the chough's strongholds today on the northwest coast of Cornwall). The female will lay between three and five eggs around April time, and both parents will provision the brood, regurgitating a mixture of invertebrate prey for them. The chicks will fledge at around six to seven weeks and these young birds will leave their parents after a further two weeks, heading off with other youngsters to create small flocks, usually elsewhere along the coast. On average a chough's life expectancy is around five to six years, but they can live until they are ten, and there has even been report of one wild bird living until it was twenty years old!

From my kneeling position, I get up ever so slightly and start to squat-walk very quietly towards where I know the pair are feeding. Choughs aren't the flightiest of birds and once they are settled you can get pretty close to them and they won't appear to be bothered in the slightest. Sometimes they will even land right in front of people, without a care in the world. But I still don't want them to fly off so am as quiet as I can be.

I reach my side of the brow and peek over the edge. There they are! Two striking birds right before my eyes! When you get a close look at a chough you can see why they were such a target for taxidermy in the past as their plumage is stunning. Their glossy black backs coupled with their red beaks and legs make them unlike any other bird in the UK, and they are nothing short of delightful!

They don't seem unnerved by me being there, so I quickly take some shots. I'm not sure how they will come out as the mizzle is now all around us and it is incredibly dark, but I try nonetheless. I watch the choughs feed for around five minutes, poking their curved red beaks into the soft soil and swallowing invertebrates, before one of them 'chee-ows' and in a flash they take off and fly back down the headland. I have heard reports of this pair having used the island for quite a while now, and, as they disappear out of view, I find myself hoping that they breed here next year.

I pick myself up off the damp ground. My face and hair are now completely wet because of the mist and I put my camera away before starting the 30-minute walk back home. When the choughs returned to Cornwall it was a huge story across the UK and even reached the national news. It also held huge significance for the people in Cornwall as these charismatic birds have been long entwined in the county's history. There is a Cornish tale that when King Arthur died he turned into a chough, and so it was bad luck to kill one. While I can't confirm the truth of this story (or even that King Arthur was real), it's true that they are a huge part of the county's identity and that everyone was thrilled when they returned! I hope that they never again disappear, and that year on year we have the privilege of seeing them flourish and thrive around our coastline, with their bright red beaks.

# AUTUMN SPECTACLES

The time is 4pm on a sunny afternoon in the middle of October, and Dave and I are driving west. As we travel down the narrow winding roads, the sun is beaming through the car window and the adjacent hedgerows filled with ivy blossom are so close to the sides of the van you could touch them. We don't think of blossom as much during the autumn months, but this is when ivy will bloom. From September through to November the plant's pale golden flower globes sprinkle hedgerows throughout the UK, in among the bramble and hawthorn. And these flowers are a vital lifeline for our pollinators at this time of year. Late butterflies, bees, wasps, moths and hoverflies all take advantage of ivy's autumnal nectar buffet. It has even been found that over 70 different pollinators species use the plant, showing that it really is of huge significance.

Wildlife watching starts earlier and earlier now. With the sun beginning to set at around 6.30pm, and with the clocks going back on the last Sunday in October, daylight hours reduce sharply as we head into winter. But it is this shift that is a factor triggering a remarkable change in our largest wild land mammal, creating one of the most magnificent autumn wildlife spectacles we have in the UK.

These mammals are a bit of a rarity in Cornwall, with strongholds on the sweeping uplands of Bodmin Moor and historically interspersed and isolated populations found towards the east of the county and into Devon. But now their numbers are increasing, and they can be seen roaming on the remote parts of the Land's End peninsula, although sightings are uncommon and you have to be pretty lucky to see one. A friend of mine, however, has given me a tip-off that she has seen them around the coast path near Saint Levan – so that is where we are headed today.

Despite the rarity of this species in Cornwall, they are by no means rare in the UK. With the latest census reporting their numbers standing at around 350,000 individuals, their conservation status is that of 'least-concern'. Their preferred habitats are upland moors, heathland and coniferous woodland, which they will make use of throughout the year at different times. Historically, they were a species of the forest, but since mass deforestation in the areas where they are found they have become accustomed to the wide open expanses of moorland throughout most of their range, heading towards whatever forest they can find or to lower ground and valleys during the winter months for more shelter. Roughly 80 per cent of the UK population are found in Scotland, and at this time of the year, if you head to the Highlands, their roars and bellows can be heard for miles.

We pull up in Porthchapel beach car park and walk down towards the beach and the coast path. As it's a beautiful afternoon we have decided to do part of the coast path walk, from Porthchapel to Porthgwarra beach. It must be around a mile, possibly less, and on a day like today I could walk ten miles in this incredible autumn sun! With the perfectly smooth towering stacks of grey prismatic granite formations standing around 60m (197ft) above sea level, it is truly otherworldly. These rocks are what this area is famous for, and they attract landscape photographers in their droves, who flock here each year from around the world to capture this part of Cornwall's outstanding beauty. We head up around the coast path, our cameras in our bags, and I look down to the turquoise-blue water below. It is almost florescent in the beaming warm sunlight as I look out to the jagged rocks where a few shags are resting with some herring gulls. Then directly in front of us I see a bird take to flight and a bright flash of white. It lands on one of the granite rocks and I can see that it's a female wheatear, with her orange-brown cheeks and smart dark-grey eye stripe. 'She must be on her way back,' I say to Dave, as this is the last we'll see of this year's wheatears before they make their long migration back to central Africa.

We've nearly reached Porthgwarra beach and, having not seen what we're after, we plan our next steps. The time is now 5.50pm. If it was the summer months we would be more than happy to carry on around the coast path, but given that the light will soon start to fade, we decide to retrace our steps. Despite knowing this route like the back of our hands, we'd rather not have to walk it at night, particularly as many parts are directly next to the cliff edge.

But then we hear an unmistakable sound. A sound that makes all of the hairs on the back of your neck stand up and a rush of adrenaline coarse through your body. The air is still and it carries far, echoing around the surrounding landscape making it even more dramatic than it already is. It is the roar of a magnificent red deer stag!

'Shit!' I say to Dave, 'Where do you think that came from?!' We look around us frantically, to see if we can spot antlers peaking up above the gorse, but we can't see a thing. We wait a further four minutes, hardly moving a muscle, and then we hear it again. And it seems to be getting closer! It sounds a little further back, towards Porthgwarra, so we decide to start walking back, trying to be as stealth-like as possible. Right now is the most dangerous time to shock a red deer stag as he will be soaring with testosterone.

Each year in October we see red deer come into their breeding season, when the males perform one of the greatest and most revered wildlife spectacles we have in this country. This is where stags battle it out in a process called rutting. When two magnificent males lock antlers they are in a fight to gain breeding rights, which sometimes leads to one of them getting severely injured. The rut is triggered by various biological and environmental factors, including the lessening in day length. As the photoperiod (the hours of daylight) becomes shorter, it creates hormonal changes within the stags, increasing their testosterone levels. The heightened level of testosterone raging through the stag's body leads to increased aggression and vocalizations, which it uses to ward off any potential rival. The animal's impressive antlers are now also fully developed, and these are shed completely each winter or early spring in a process called antler casting. Stags will begin to grow a new pair around April, and through the summer months, particularly July, the antlers will grow at their fastest rate, as the stags take full advantage of the abundance of lush and tasty resources that summer brings. By late summer the antlers are fully grown, and the stag will begin to shed the antler velvet, a type of soft, furry skin that supplies blood and nutrients to the antlers as they grow. Antlers are an extension of the skull and are the fastest-growing mammal tissue on planet Earth, which is pretty impressive in itself! Female red deer (called hinds) also go into oestrus (that is, heat) during the same period, and the smell of a receptive female can further stimulate the male's desire to breed. If you have watched red stags at this time of year you will have noticed them constantly sniffing the air and often drooling as they catch a scent of a receptive female. Just like the lads in Newquay on a Friday night. Delightful.

Red deer populations across the UK may rut at varying different times, but most activity will peak around October, although studies have found that rutting is beginning slightly earlier now, possibly due to climate change. The best time to see this extraordinary display is at dusk or dawn, but always remember to stay well back. Red deer stags weigh in at around 200kg (440lb 15oz), and stand at roughly 1.2m (4ft) at the shoulder, with their mighty antlers weighing up to 15kg (33lb 1oz). This is when they are at their most volatile, so remember to admire them from afar!

We turn the corner along the coast path and look up ahead. And then we see him! Standing tall among the gorse bushes in all of his majesty, a regal sight against the fading sunlight, is a glorious red deer stag. And my goodness is he a looker! His antlers are in perfect condition, his fur a deep russet-brown, and he has a knowing glint in his eyes. It's as if he is aware of how handsome he is – and that he is the king of this part of Cornwall.

As we drop to the ground my heart is racing. The stag is still quite far away but we don't dare get any closer as we don't want to disturb him – or upset him! But in the time it takes me to get hold of my camera and look back up he is gone, just as suddenly as he appeared. We stay on the ground for another ten minutes, then we hear another bellow, but now it sounds a lot further away. He has probably headed back onto the heathland, looking for a fight.

I pack away my camera. The time is now 6.20pm. Very soon the light will be gone so we decide to take a brisk walk along the coast path so that we don't get caught out by the fading sun. Today wasn't my day to get a shot of a red deer stag in Cornwall, but I wasn't really expecting it given that they're a rarity here. He was still extraordinary to see. I will have to try again next year to capture the red deer rut here in Cornwall, one of nature's greatest and most magnificent autumn spectacles.

# THE KILL

The comma has to be one of the most inconspicuous butterfly species in the UK, especially in the autumn months. Their name is derived from the distinctive white marking on the underside of their wings that resembles a comma, and their scalloped wings and cryptic orange-brown colouration make them true masters of disguise. And when they are resting in a pile of old leaves or on a tree branch, they are impeccably camouflaged. The comma butterfly I'm looking at now, however, is quite easy to see as it is feeding on some of the blackberries that have started to turn in the hedgerow next to me. At this time of year commas can often be seen feeding off rotting fruit as it is packed with sugary goodness: a butterfly's dream! They are a butterfly species that you can see right the way through the year. On warm winter days they will often awaken from their hibernation to have a flutter around in search of food, but they will fully emerge the following spring, around March.

I watch the comma for a few moments using its long proboscis to enjoy the blackberries as a clattering of jackdaws flies overhead – clattering being the collective name for a group of these birds, the smallest corvid in the UK. I listen as their raspy flight calls fill the air and I hear a great tit singing its alarm, 'seee-seee', possibly due to my presence, or that of the jackdaws, or perhaps both. The largest tit species in the UK, great tits have quite the reputation as the bullies of the bird feeder, and will act with aggression to get the feeder for themselves. But they have an incredible vocal repertoire, having around 40 different calls, the most commonly heard and famous being the two repeated high and low notes that resemble 'tea-cher, tea-tea-cher'. I can also hear house sparrows, blackbirds, chaffinch and the 'tic-tic-tic' alarm call of a robin.

So on this warm October afternoon, as I head down into one of my favourite wildlife valleys in Cornwall, I have a good feeling that I might spot something exciting today. The air just feels alive.

I open the clasp on the gate and close it behind me so that the horses don't attempt to follow, then sit down on the dark shaded narrow path and pull out my ghillie suit. Before I enter the fields I always put my ghillie suit on and the camo shield on my camera, as past experience tells me that from now on anything could appear! I need to be ready and as camouflaged as possible, just in case. Once in my full sniper outfit, I walk down and into the bottom fields and look out across the valley, the auburn tones of autumn now in full swing, and head across into the second field to the hide.

My mate Dave and I built this hide from scratch earlier on in the year. It was around April time, for our Cornwall Wildlife Safari, when we discovered that it was an excellent place to spot badgers, foxes and roe deer. Made with wood and sealed with waterproof camo green paint, it has a cut-out area the whole way round, with camo netting secured to the open lookout areas, so that anyone in the hide remains as concealed and camouflaged as possible. I mean, it is pretty basic, and certainly won't be winning any awards for its innovative architectural design, but it does the job. I had always had fantastic wildlife encounters in these fields, but since building the hide they have become even better! The week-long planning, bickering and building of the hide by hand was more than worthwhile!

'Nothing yet,' I whisper to myself as I take our makeshift wooden door off and kneel down, sliding my body and camera bag across the plywood floor. The hide is big enough so that you can sit quite comfortably, but the roof is still close to your head. I'm not entirely sure if someone over six foot would fit in it, but being a tiny human, it is perfect for me. I sit and wait, looking out in front of me, and watch a pair of jays flying through the trees of the valley, and rabbits feeding and jumping around along the field margins. It is warm, it is still and it is bright – the perfect evening for wildlife.

I sit there for over an hour and nothing appears. Although it is one of my most reliable wildlife spots in the county, I will quite often sit here for hours until it is completely dark and not see a thing. But this is why, when you *do* spot something, it is all the more special, especially when it comes to British wildlife *actually* in the wild. As much as we love our native species, they do have a reputation the world over of being notoriously difficult to film.

I lift up the camo netting, peeking through to see if anything is around, and then I turn back into the hide. I see a large, bright white bird that is very close but is obscured by the netting. What I initially think is a herring gull has landed in the field. The bird is standing motionless but then it pulls at something before moving back up into its standing position. It's feeding, I think to myself. Without moving the netting, I position my eye to look through one of the gaps to try to get a better look at whatever this gull is up to, but, as I do so, I can't believe my eyes. The bright white chest is surrounded by dappled brown plumage, and it has piercing auburn eyes and a bright yellow beak with a sharp black tip. I quickly realize that it isn't a herring gull at all: it's a buzzard! And it's a buzzard with a kill! It is also ginormous!

'Oh God!' I say under my breath in a frantic whisper as I turn to grab my camera. I have never seen a buzzard with a kill so unbelievably close and think to myself: these really will be the shots of all shots! I get my camera into position and turn my body round as I start to lift back the netting over my camera. But as I do, one of the legs of my tripod drops. I hadn't fastened it tight enough, so, just as I lift the netting there is a sudden jerky movement as the camera falls slightly. The buzzard looks up, directly at me, a pair of sharp intense eyes looking straight into mine, as if the raptor is staring straight into my soul. In a matter of seconds its huge wings spread and it takes to flight, carrying its prey within its bright yellow talons. 'It's killed a pigeon!' I say to myself.

Buzzards are known to be scavengers, which is why you will often see them on the side of the road taking advantage of carrion killed by passing vehicles. But the buzzard's diet is very varied, and they are more of an opportunistic and generalist predator. And it is these feeding behaviours that have played an important role in the species' comeback. Once a fairly common bird in the UK, they were targeted by relentless persecution from landowners who assumed that buzzards threated their game birds, leading the population to fall to as few as one thousand breeding pairs in the 1900s. Coupled with the intense use of pesticides that killed their prey, and then the spread of myxomatosis in 1953, which was believed to have killed off 99 per cent of our rabbit population (a favoured prey of these birds), our common buzzards became not so common. But thanks to stringent legal protection and changes in farming practices the buzzard is now quite the conservation success story, with numbers quadrupling since the 1970s. They can now be found nesting in every county in the UK.

Their speedy recovery can be attributed in large part to their varied diet, which has played a major factor. They will utilize any feeding opportunity should it arise. They predate rabbits, small mammals and small to medium-sized birds, but if resources are low, they will eat invertebrates, with earthworms making up a large part of their diet, and they have also been known to take reptiles and amphibians. To locate their prey they will either soar up high, scanning the ground below, or will use a perch of some sort – a tree, a building or a telegraph pole – anywhere that gives them a view from where they can stealthily fly towards their prey, talons first. Behind the hide there is a thick row of woodland and also some telegraph poles. Could this buzzard have been perched up there and seen this pigeon on the ground, taking the opportunity to kill when the time was right? Highly likely!

I scan the field margins hoping to catch a glimpse and praying that the buzzard hasn't flown out of view completely. As I look to the far right-hand side at the base of the hedgerow I see a flurry of white feathers being feverishly plucked in clumps and blowing around in the slight breeze. 'It's still here!' I mutter. But the hedgerow is far away and that, coupled with the long grass, means that I can only vaguely see the top of the buzzard's head occasionally poking up. So, in a split second I decide to leave the hide. I hurl open the door and throw my body onto the ground face first, in my full ghillie suit with the hood up. I then proceed to slide across the field on my stomach, commando crawling, holding my camera above my head. God, I feel like a dickhead, I think, as I slither along at a snail's pace. If only people knew what I get up to in Cornish valleys.

Eventually I get close enough to the buzzard that I can see its full face as it pulls up its neck, with a beak full of pigeon. I'm still very far away, but don't want to get any closer – I don't want to disturb it, especially while it's having its dinner (as let's face it, no one likes to be interrupted when they're eating!). But from here I can appreciate its full size and power. With a wingspan of roughly 1.4m (4½ft), and weighing up to 1.4kg (3lb 1oz), they are sizeable birds. As in most raptor species, the female is slightly bigger than the male, yet all buzzards have highly variable plumage. Some are almost completely brown, while others are more dappled white or even nearly pure white, which can often lead to misidentification. I'm not sure if this bird is a male or a female, but either way, it seems huge!

I pull my body up to a crouching position in the grass and point my camera straight at the buzzard with its kill. I put my shutter speed up high as I'm hopeful I'll be able to capture some of the flurry of feathers swirling around as the buzzard looks up from its prey. Then I hold my finger down and take some shots. The buzzard doesn't seem at all fazed by my presence, probably because I'm in camo. It stays there feeding for around ten minutes until it has devoured the pigeon, before spreading its wings and flying into the woodlands below.

Once it is finally and safely out of view I stand up off the ground, every bone and muscle stiff from holding the same position, and walk over to where it was feeding. I look down and there is nothing but a pile of feathers remaining. I pick one up and twizzle it round in my fingers. It still feels warm, and the end of the calamus (the quill), which leads up into the rachis (the central shaft), is still in perfect condition, having been plucked out with clear precision. This is a tell-tale sign of a raptor kill, and a great way of working out if you have birds of prey in your area rather than, say, a fox. When you next come across a pile of feathers on a nature walk look at the ends. If the quill has been plucked it is a bird of prey kill, but if the end of the quill is broken it will most likely be a fox kill. Raptors pluck whereas foxes tear.

I sit back down on the ground and flick through my photos as dusk begins to fall. I did get some shots, but will have to have a proper look when I get home as the buzzard was very far away, and I don't think I got the shot of all shots. Nonetheless, what an incredible wildlife encounter to have had on this warm October evening. To see buzzards thriving once again in the great British countryside is a wonderful thing, and never in a million years did I think I would see one today on the ground feeding! Very happy with my wildlife spotting, I start to walk back home. To have seen a buzzard with a fresh kill: well, it doesn't get much better than that!

# November

# WINTER SPECIALITIES

The time is 3.30pm. And it feels as if winter has arrived in Cornwall. The grey, low-hanging clouds are thick and moist as I see a skein of geese flying overhead. The beech trees that surround me are awash with their orange-red leaves and the forest floor is speckled with acorns that have fallen from the ancient oaks that are peppered in between the beech, like a group of old friends. The golden hues of autumn are still clinging on – not quite ready to leave us just yet. From behind the base of a tree I see a grey squirrel pop out with two acorns in its mouth. It then turns away and dashes off, leaping across the leaf litter and out of sight, clearly on its way to add them to its precious winter store. I bend down to pick up an acorn, as I like to fill my coat pockets with forest finds that I then inspect at home. I see a vibrant deep-purple fungus, standing around 10cm (4in) tall and with its striking gills underneath. It's one of my favourite fungi, an amethyst deceiver. This fungus is often found from late summer through to November at the base of beech trees, but it can also be found in mixed woodland across the UK. Their extraordinary-looking fruiting bodies are like something out of a storybook, and their bright purple colour against the oranges of the forest is simply a feast for the eyes at this time of the year!

November may seem like a month when wildlife in the UK slows down. Our dormice head into hibernation, finding the base of an old tree to make a simple woven nest out of grass; and our bats head to their hibernacula, where they go into a state of torpor, mostly in old buildings, trees and caves. The much-loved hedgehog finds somewhere safe to sleep for the duration of the winter, leading wildlife lovers to once again plead with the nation to check their bonfires before lighting them on 5 November (something that we have to do every year).

Yet in among the steady decline in activity for a number of species, there are others that are preparing for a busy winter season ahead, with many just arriving. Our wetlands welcome a new colour palette of feathers, as our numbers of widgeon, teal, dunlin and oystercatcher swell as resident populations are joined by overwintering migrants. Otters become easier to spot down by the edges of lakes, rivers and estuaries at dawn and dusk due to the reduced vegetation cover, and kingfishers stand out among the bulrushes like colourful beacons of light! Knots perform one of the greatest winter wildlife spectacles in the UK when they are seen in their thousands at high-tide roosts, their white and silver bodies twisting and turning as one. Our woodlands become filled with brambling that have travelled to the UK to escape the harsh winters of Russia and Scandinavia, and, if we are lucky, it might even be a waxwing year! Still, to this day, I don't think these birds look real, with their pinkish plumage, glorious head crest, and yellow and red feathers. It's as if they have been painted. And if we are lucky enough to have an influx of these magnificent birds during the colder months, known as an 'irruption year', the best place to try to spot them is in your local supermarket car park. For some reason, across the UK, this is where rowan trees have been planted, and rowan berries are one of the waxwing's favourite foods!

Winter is a spectacular season for wildlife here, which is all the more reason to put on our wellies and get outside.

I walk down the path surrounded by golden leaves, listening out for the bird I want to photograph today. I have been hearing them the past few weeks; in fact I heard my first ones a few weeks ago in October just after the sun had set and I was walking home one evening with Isabelle. Their very distinctive 'tsee-tsee' calls filled the air under the cover of darkness, and I thought to myself that they must be just arriving. Unlike our hirundine species and swifts, which will feed on the wing and so migrate by day, many of our birds, such as starlings and warblers, will migrate by night, meaning they are less susceptible to predation and use less energy given the cooler night-time conditions. The bird I'm looking for today does exactly this, making its way across the North Sea from Scandinavia each autumn to spend the winter with us, with most of its migration done by night.

My feet crunch the fallen leaves with each step as I head to the edge of the woodland and towards the hedgerow, which is the perfect habitat for it. In early November our hedgerows are still laden with hawthorn berries, one of the favourite food sources of these birds. Yet as we head through winter and berry supply diminishes, thanks to the number of species that feed on them, they will head to ground to eat earthworms and any other tasty invertebrates they can find. In recent years they have been spotted more frequently in people's gardens, attracted by old fruit left out for blackbirds, and they will also feed on bird seed left on the ground. Orchards, with their abundance of old rotting fruit, are also a magnet for them. But today I'm hoping to capture one feeding on hawthorn along the hedgerow, ideally with a berry in its mouth. Since I've only ever been able to capture one photograph like this before – a blackcap feeding on ivy berries one January along the hedgerows of the Gannel estuary – this is somewhat unlikely, and even then, it wasn't my finest work. But I have a saying when it comes to British wildlife: you've got to be in it to win it!

I sit down on the ground along the woodland edge, the hedgerow in front of me on the other side of the road. As I have my 100–500mm lens on my camera body, if I crossed the road I would actually be too close to photograph anything. Plus, standing in the middle of a tiny windy Cornish road with blind spots in each direction is never a good idea, and one I would strongly advise against. So I sit in among the leaf litter, the dampness of the woodland understory seeping through my leggings and making my bottom cold and wet. Oh well, I say to myself, at least I won't be hit by a car. I'll take a wet bottom any day of the week!

And then a little further along the hedgerow from where I am, I spot one! I knew they would be here! I see it, flitting in and out of the hawthorn-berry-laden branches, with its brown back and head plumage, the prominent white stripe above the eye creating the perfect rock-star make-up. The white chest is dappled with brown flecks and just under the wings on either side is that famous patch of orange-red plumage, which is where they get their name from. It's a redwing! And my first of the season!

Redwings are the smallest of our six true thrush species here in the UK. With a wingspan of just 35cm (13¾in) and weighing between 50g (1¾oz) and 75g (2¾oz) compared to our largest, the mistle thrush, which has a wingspan of roughly 48cm (19in) and can weigh as much as 150g (5½oz), redwings are tiny. We have three resident species of thrush in the UK: the blackbird, the song thrush and the mistle thrush. Then we also have the ring ouzel, our only summer migrant thrush species, which comes to the UK each year around March in order to breed, primarily in the uplands of the north and in Scotland, and then leaves our shores again in the autumn. Redwings are one of our winter thrush species, along with the fieldfare, and they can often be mistaken for one another because they look quite similar and arrive here at the same time. But fieldfares are a lot larger than redwings, more on a par with the mistle thrush, and they have blue-grey head plumage and lack the distinctive wing patches of the redwing. It's said that redwings will gather towards the coastlines of Scandinavia in groups before making the mammoth journey across the North Sea to the UK, and when they arrive they will often travel around in small flocks, so if you see one always keep your eyes out for more!

I might just be in luck here, I say to myself, as my body tenses up and I hover my finger over the camera trigger. I see more redwings along the hedgerow, and they are moving up towards me, feeding on the delicious hawthorn berries as they go. I stay completely still and wait in the hope that one will land directly in front of me on the patch of berries just across the road. I've already checked my camera focus on this patch so if one lands just here to feed, it really would be the perfect shot.

But just as they move closer and I press my eye into the viewfinder, a van comes speeding along around the corner, music blaring and definitely not going at 20 miles per hour, which it should be along this stretch – it is bombing along at more like 50! Now redwings aren't the flightiest of birds, but, given the size of the road and how big, fast and loud the van is, as it speeds past all of the redwings take to flight. And as I watch them fly off into the distance and the music from the van fades away into the Cornish country lane I'm a bit miffed, to say the least. Why on earth people drive like that here is utterly beyond me. They aren't just a danger to themselves and those around them, they are also a huge danger to our wildlife.

I sit for a further half an hour, my bottom and most of my legs now completely soaked, in the hope that the birds will come back. But sadly they don't and today simply wasn't my day to photograph them. But at least I got some great views, and they won't be leaving the UK until around March next year, so I still have plenty of time to try to photograph some redwings; a real winter speciality.

# RIGHT UNDER OUR NOSES

Humans have lived alongside wildlife for as long as we have had the ability to document our time on planet Earth. Dating back to the emergence of early *Homo* species, such as *Homo erectus* and *Homo habilis*, who lived around two million years ago, animals have been entwined in our lives for as long as we have existed. These early humans were hunter-gatherers and relied on the natural environment for their food, shelter and other resources.

Archaeological and paleontological findings have provided insights into the coexistence of early humans with various forms of wildlife. The use of ancient tools alongside fossilized remains of animals found at archaeological sites demonstrate that early humans hunted and utilized animals for their survival. When we look at the cave paintings and rock art created by our past ancestors, many feature some sort of wildlife, such as those in Lascaux in France dating back between 15,000 and 17,000 years; Bhimbetka in India dating back some 30,000 years; and those in Indonesia, which are now considered to be the most ancient discovered in the world, at an estimated 44,000 years old. All these provide clear evidence through the portrayal of simple stories that humans have interacted with wildlife throughout our existence.

When the domestication of wild ruminant species (species of the hoofed variety) began some 10,000 years ago, this changed the path of our species forever. The ability to travel long distances and to carry more goods than was possible on foot opened up trade routes, thus increasing the movement of people and animals. But animal domestication and the development of farming practices also led to more settled ways of life, and the growth of hamlets, then villages, then towns. More food in turn meant more people, and the development of agriculture and the domestication of wild plants and animals were the most significant period in early human history.

As early humans adapted their way of life there were certain wild species that, without domestication, adapted to live alongside us. A study from the University of Colorado at Boulder in 2018 found that the barn swallow, for example, was able to increase its range and population numbers when humans started to construct buildings, evolving alongside us. The evolution of certain species such as urban red foxes is also being sped up by human action, so much so that, as we saw earlier, their skull and snouts are changing shape to adapt more closely to the human environment. The peppered moth changed the colour of its wings from speckled white and black, which made them perfectly camouflaged against lichen-filled trees, to pure black in the period of the Industrial Revolution so that they would remain camouflaged on trees that were now covered in soot. It's even thought that our city-dwelling blackbirds could be evolving into a separate species from their rural counterparts, as they have stouter and shorter beaks and sing at different pitches to counteract background noise, often in the dead of night. Human impact on wildlife all around the world is perpetual.

But some small, opportunist species latched onto this new human way of life and hid in plain sight, taking advantage of our growing food supply, waste products and warm buildings. They adapted to live alongside us and, by using our resources, expanded their own populations rapidly, which inevitably led to some individuals travelling around the world as hidden stowaways. Having reached Europe some 3,000 years ago from their native southwest Asia, or perhaps even earlier, they eventually reached the UK.

The species that I want to photograph tonight did just that. It's a pioneering, fluffy mammal, with black beady eyes and a pink nose, one that continues to live alongside us the world over.

'Are you there?' I shout after banging on the door for three minutes. 'It's bloody Baltic out here, come on!' Dave finally comes. to his front door and Isabelle bolts in. She knows that her uncle Dave has ample snacks downstairs and a draw full of soft squeaky toys so she loves coming round. 'Sorry,' he says, 'I was out the back.' The time is 7.30pm and I step into his warm porch from the cold winter night, leaving the twinkling star-filled night sky behind me as I close the door.

I head through the house and into the garage. As I switch on the light I can see my breath in the air. It really is cold tonight, and I can understand why this species has decided to make its home in a cosy garage in Newquay; I wouldn't like to be out in the wilds today either! This is where Dave's been seeing them and their droppings. He even found one in his bag of birdseed when he went to top up his feeders! Apparently it was just sitting in the bag, brazenly feeding in the middle of the day.

Up on the shelf I see some evidence: droppings! Tiny black poo that almost resembles grains of rice measuring around 3mm (⅛in) in length and scattered across one of the worktops in among the tools and cleaning products. 'Fabulous!' I say to myself. Now for most people the sight of these droppings would not bring them a rush of anticipation or excitement – but I'm elated, as this species is very difficult to see, let alone photograph. Given their mostly nocturnal habits, their size, at a mere 7cm (2¾in) to 9cm (3½in) in length, and their ability to hide away, we very rarely see them despite living alongside them for thousands of years.

I look around the shelf and set up my old Nikon with remote trigger and flashes on one of the corners. There seems to be a trail of droppings coming from a small space between some of the objects, so I test the focus and frame the camera up to take some shots at that position. Once I'm happy with my set-up, I leave the garage and go back through the house, telling Dave I'll be over in the morning. Isabelle and I head back out into the chilly night and on our way home. I look to Isabelle and say, as we are walking, 'You never know, we might even photograph more than one!'

These small mammals have a short lifespan, averaging around one year. But during that year, they are busy. Females that live in urban areas and are hidden away in our garages and homes have the ability to reproduce all year round, given the warmth, food resources and safety that our human-made structures provide. Females will construct a small nest out of twigs, leaves and moss in the wilds, but urban dwellers will use just about anything including cardboard, old newspaper, foam, material and even electrical cabling. Chewing through electrical cabling for many animals would be a tricky task at best, but given this animal's sharp incisors, which never stop growing, they can chew through just about anything. Wild-living individuals may reproduce less, but as litters can have between five and eight young born each month, that is still a lot of babies! And this rampant rate of reproduction, coupled with the fact that they are active throughout the year and do not hibernate, has contributed significantly to their success. After roughly 21 days the babies, which are born pink and helpless, will have developed their full fur, and be weaned off their mother's milk and eating solid foods. However, not many of these young ones will make it to a year old. This species is a major food source for foxes, barn owls, kestrels, stoats and weasels, as well as often being predated by our domesticated cats and dogs.

It's 8.30am the next morning when I bang on the door. Dave opens it, I say hello, and then as fast as I can head to the garage to see if my camera has captured anything overnight. I woke up at 6am this morning and all I've been thinking about since is if I've managed to get a shot, one that I have always wanted: and it would be my first!

I enter the garage and grab my old Nikon. I frantically flick through the photos; the first ones just look like a blurry pink tail. Perhaps my assumptions about where they might appear were wrong because, from what I've captured so far, they seem to be coming from the sides. But then I get to it – the shot I have always wanted! Its tiny, pointed face is peeking out, with its long whiskers and large fur-covered ears, greyish-brown all over and those gorgeous black-pin shiny eyes: it's a house mouse!

House mice can be found throughout the UK and, as one of the most abundant mammals, are far from a rarity. Out of our six species of mice, the house mouse, along with the wood mouse, is the most common. These two species can often be hard to differentiate as they are quite similar in appearance, but the house mouse is greyer than the sandy-brown wood mouse, which also has lighter fur underneath. Other UK species of mice – the yellow-necked mouse, the harvest mouse, the dormouse and the edible dormouse – are even harder to see (this last-named being a non-native species that escaped from a private collection in Hertfordshire in 1902). Dormice aren't in fact true mice, but are part of a separate family, although they are still classified as rodents as are squirrels and beavers.

'Yes!' I say to myself, as I pack away my camera equipment and run back through the house to show Dave. I'm over the moon that I managed to capture one. Despite being one of our most common species, they are still a delight to see! And you have to hand it to the house mouse. From humble beginnings in southwest Asia thousands of years ago to becoming one of the world's most successful mammals, they've done pretty well. Thanks to their adaptability to new environments and food sources, and their ability to hide away, this species will continue to thrive alongside us. Even if we cannot see them, they are always there, right under our noses.

# TEASELS AND JAM

Tall, tapering russet-brown stems fill the surrounding meadow, laden with thick, crinkly seed heads and touched with a delicate cloaking of frost. I see a patch of vibrant crimson-red carapaces. Hidden away, and speckled with tiny black spots in among the auburn icy jungle, they appear minuscule from where I'm standing, but, once I've noticed them, I can't look away. I walk slightly closer and stretch out my hand, parting the compact seed clusters ever so softly as I don't want any of them to fall to the frosty ground: a mass of scarlet and ebony beetles all huddled together, seeking refuge from the cold winter's air.

They are seven-spot ladybirds, and hundreds of them! Each and every one is a tiny masterpiece, and together a loveliness.

A 'loveliness' is the collective name of a group of ladybirds, and during the winter months they will often head into hibernation together, finding sheltered nooks and crannies to hide away in, using the crevices in tree bark, old rotting wood, somewhere warm in people's homes, or the hollow stems and seed heads of plants, just like this curled dock plant. They will hunker down for the duration of winter and emerge again the following spring. Sometimes they will be found in small groups of just two or three, but they can also be found in groups of hundreds, or even thousands of individuals. This, of course, provides them with protection from predation as well as additional shelter from the cold, and they are also one of my favourite things to find when out on a winter walk – a loveliness in more than one sense of the word.

But today I have come to this winter meadow in the hope of seeing one of our most colourful garden bird species, as these meadows are perfect for them at this time of year. They too have a rather wonderful collective name: a 'charm'.

I carry on down the muddy path, which is hard in some places due to the frost overnight, yet the warm winter sun has started to heat the ground slightly, and my wellies make the odd squelch here and there in the defrosted patches along the way. This area in spring and summer was a bustling metropolis of colour and life, yet now, with the long grasses having turned shades of gold and brown and the trees along the meadow's edges having lost their leaves, it is a rather monotone landscape. At first glance the surrounding area may seem devoid of wildlife, but a winter wildflower meadow is just as important and brimming with species as it is in summer. Queen bumblebees will be asleep beneath my feet, the grassy tussocks and hollow stems will be filled with caterpillars and chrysalises, toads will be hibernating under piles of old wood, and now is the best time of year to find harvest mice nests. This species does not hibernate but will lessen their activity during the winter months. Look out for small woven grass cups usually at the bases of the thickest tussocks.

Not cutting back meadows in the autumn is one of the most important things we can do to help our wildlife here in the UK. Habitats are vital for biodiversity and supply ample food for many species that are still active in this period. Each side of the path in between the grasses, seed heads litter the landscape as far as the eye can see: rounded knapweed and burdock with their rounded and spiky appearance, embellished with a dusting of frost; poppy heads with their globe-like clusters, accentuated at the top with what look like icy stars; and wild angelica, with delicate feathery tops and slender tall stems that appear to have tiny crystals all over them, like frosty winter sculptures. All of these seed-bearing wild plants will be a lifeline throughout the winter months for many different species. Small mammals will take advantage of their tasty and calorific offerings, as will our birds, and during the winter you can see linnets, bullfinch, house sparrows and yellowhammers feeding on them.

Just in front of me on the brow of the meadow, standing like spiky beacons in the winter sunlight, are a patch of a native wild plant. During the winter months these are the favourite food source of the bird I want to photograph today, so I make my way over to them. The humble teasel.

Teasels are biennial plants that are famous for their tall spiky stems and distinctive purple flowers that can be seen through July and August. They are steeped with history in this country and were used as an essential part of our textile industry for many years. The spiky flower heads were a vital tool, particularly during the 19th century, and were used to tease and comb wool before spinning it, a process called 'teasing' or 'carding', hence the name 'teasel'. During the summer months their purple flower heads are an excellent food source for pollinators and their seeds during the winter are a delicious treat for many finch species. But they are a favourite of one bird in particular.

I take my camera out of my bag and extend the tripod's legs. I haven't brought anything to sit on today and, given how cold the ground is, I don't really fancy getting a freezing bum. It's around 10.30 in the morning and I have a few hours before I have to be back home for a meeting at 3pm, so I decide I'll spend a few hours here, waiting. I see these birds often at this spot and, as their favourite food is in front of me and it is a sunny day, I hedge my bets that they should appear at some point.

Thankfully, these beautiful birds have been doing well across the country in recent years. They experienced a sharp decline in the 1970s and 1980s, which can be attributed to the use of pesticides and changes in farming practices. This greatly reduced the abundance of 'weeds' (wild native plants to you and me) so that they had less to eat, leading to a drastic population decline. But thanks to more sympathetic farming practices, and the fact that they've benefited hugely from our garden feeders (niger seed is one of their favourites), they are now a green-listed species, with some 1.7 million breeding pairs. They are highly sociable birds and will often nest in lose colonies, with nesting areas mostly in hedgerows or thick scrub around a metre off the ground. During the winter they move around largely in flocks, sometimes of just a few individuals, but other groups are in their hundreds, and it's these flocks that are called a charm.

Then I hear them. And they are close by! There are most definitely a few of them! It's a crisp and tinkling call that I have always thought sounds slightly electronic, somehow, a series of raspy whistling notes and rattling trills. It is wonderful!

I frame my camera on the teasels, saying to myself: surely they will land over there. And then I see my first one. The bright red face and white and black head, the sandy-brown chest and black plumage with a gleaming white underside and the prominent black wings with a streak of yellow all make it stand out like a shining ball of colour against the winter landscape.

It's a goldfinch!

I hold my finger down on the trigger as it begins to feed on the teasels. Goldfinch, like all finches in the UK, are primarily seed eaters. During the spring and summer months they will eat a variety of insects and invertebrates as well, and it is these that they will feed to their young. But goldfinch have a specially adapted, almost tweezer-like beak that enables them to reach the winter seeds of plants that other birds struggle to reach, which is why teasels are among their most important food sources. I zoom in as far my lens allows to see if it's a male or female. Goldfinches lack any real sexual dimorphism, but if you manage to get a closer look you can differentiate them. They have a nickname in the UK – 'jam-faces' – as their distinctive red facial patch makes them look as if they've been dipping their faces in jam. But these red patches also help to sex a goldfinch. In the male, the red patch will extend behind the eye, whereas in the female it will stop just before the eye. Another way to tell the difference is by looking at their rictal bristles, tiny whiskers that many birds have at the tops of their beaks. In goldfinch, the male's rictal bristles are black whereas the female's are more brown-grey. This way of sexing a goldfinch can only really be done on exceptionally close inspection, however, so I would stick to looking at the jam!

This one is definitely a male and I manage to get some really close-up shots before, in a flash, he hears the rest of the charm flying overhead and spreads his wings to go and join them. The time is now 2pm and I must head back for my meeting, although on a winter's day like today I could quite happily stay in this meadow until the sun sets!

Goldfinches have to be one of the most attractive birds we have here, and now, thanks to their increasing numbers, they can be seen right across Britain, apart from the remote Highlands of Scotland. And it is wonderful to see them thrive once more, which is just how it should be. They are also one of my favourite birds to photograph, especially in winter. The perfect mixture of teasels and jam!

# December

# BIG WINGS OF NEW ENGLAND

The cold air hammers against my skin. The wind is so strong that it feels as if it could lift me into the air or knock me down to the ground should I stumble. It's like I'm heading into battle – battle with the North Atlantic Ocean. The waves are ferociously crashing against the coastal cliffs, raw, brutal and unpredictable. It's almost as if the ocean itself is sending a stark warning to any passers-by with its roaring thunderous swell: 'mess with me if you dare'.

Welcome to the Cornish coastline, in December.

At this time of year, and especially on a day like today, I have the entire coast path to myself. I look for miles in front of me and miles behind and there isn't another single soul. The conditions are so bad that I can't even see any seabirds, and I think I must be the only person mad enough to come out on such a day. But with good reason, as early this morning I had a tip-off that one of the world's most extraordinary marine mammals has been seen just south of the stretch that I'm walking on: a species that can be found in all oceans around the world, but one that I have never seen before. Sightings of them are still a rarity in Cornwall, but during our winter months reports of them are increasing. So I thought to myself it's worth a shot, right?

These magnificent animals are now increasing around the world, after experiencing an estimated 95 per cent drop in population numbers over the course of the 20th century due to a sharp increase in hunting at the beginning of the 1900s. Indeed, our history with this species is a grave one. Beginning as early as the 16th century, but escalating through the 17th and peaking during the 18th and 19th centuries, these creatures were extensively hunted for their valuable blubber and baleen. The blubber, when rendered into oil, was a valuable commodity, used around the world for lighting lamps and for soap and candle production. As a lubricant it was used in the production of firearms as it helped to prevent corrosion and sustained smooth functioning of mechanisms, and it was widely used in both world wars. It was also used in leather clothing, submarine and aircraft engines, automobiles and explosives, and even in textile mills. In fact, we used the oil in pretty much everything. In addition, baleen was used to make umbrella ribs, corsets, fishing rods, baskets, hoops for skirts, and even carriage springs, and bone was used to carve sculptures.

Some countries ate the meat of these animals, as some still do today, and the industry concerned was both ruthless and relentless. Ships would voyage to every corner of the ocean in order to harvest them. Then, with the advent of harpoon technology during the 18th and 19th centuries, the hunting of these gentle giants intensified. Harpoons had barbed heads and were shot with an explosive charge created by gunpowder, which was enough to penetrate the creature's skin and kill on impact or to render them unconscious and unrecoverable. It's a horrifying image that still makes my eyes water. By the mid-20th century this species faced the imminent threat of extinction.

Thankfully, regulation that came into effect in 1985 established a moratorium on the hunting of these animals for commercial use, leading to a substantial decline in their killing. Yet practices vary from one country to another, so they remain a species of conservation concern and one that requires continued monitoring.

Since 2019 Cornwall Wildlife Trust has recorded more than 75 sightings around our coastline, and by the summer of 2023 a total of 29 sightings had been added to the list! The fact that one of these was in June, off the coast of Falmouth, and only the second sighting during the summer months, is another sign that the species is in recovery and that their numbers are increasing. Most sightings have been from the period December to March while they are on their migration routes – from feeding to breeding grounds – but numbers are increasing year on year. Of course, populations are starting to recover, which is a major reason for the increased sightings. But, given advancements in technology, and the fact that most people now have easy access to a camera phone, more sightings are being recorded, as ordinary people spot them out at sea by chance. It's actually fantastic: citizen science on the go!

I find a semi-sheltered inlet in a cove area between two headlands, with the old stone-wall embankment providing me with a small, yet very welcome, break from being battered by the wind. I sit there for a moment to gather myself, hunkering down amid the bouncy grass, and decide not to take my camera out of my bag unless I see some signs. The wind today must be at least 35 miles per hour and, to be honest, it was a bit silly of me to come out. But I'm desperate to try to see one of these creatures. In the last week or so I have seen other people's phone footage all over social media. These animals have been scattered up and down the coast, and I know that today is a long shot at best – but you just never know!

About half an hour goes by and I'm getting substantially colder. This really wasn't my finest idea. But as I look out to the water I see what I think is a large splash – one that was out of the ordinary and that, even in these rough seas, stood out. I squint as I try to focus, then I see what I read as a dark grey hump, like a rock protruding from the ocean, but it disappears again in an instant. 'Could it be?' I say to myself as I scramble to pull my camera out of my bag, hopeful that it is. Could it be a humpback whale?!

Humpback whales are among the largest whales in the world. They are part of the mysticetes, the largest group of baleen whales that includes the largest animal ever known to live on Earth – the blue whale. But humpbacks, reaching roughly between 12m (39½ft) and 18m (59ft) and weighing up to 40 tons when fully grown, are still a very impressive size! Their pectoral fins alone can grow to nearly 4.9m (16ft) and this is where their Latin name comes from, *Megaptera novaeangliae*, 'big wing of New England', which is where they were first documented by European whalers.

Mysticetes split from odontocetes (toothed species such as killer whales, dolphins and porpoises, narwhals and sperm whales) around 39 million years ago, with the first known whale-like creature appearing in the fossil record 52.5 million years ago. And over the course of their millions of years of evolution, coupled with their lifespan, with some humpbacks living up to the age of 50, they have become true masters of their environment.

Known to be highly vocal creatures they are famous for their 'singing'. They are able to produce a complex series of haunting moans, grunts and almost shriek-like calls, which can be heard under the water for several thousand miles. It has even been found that calves 'whisper' to their mothers in a quiet tone of grunts and squeaks. A highly transient species, they migrate each year, with some populations migrating from the high polar regions that supply them with nutrient-dense feeding grounds and returning to their breeding grounds close to the equator each and every year.

Their migration spans some 5,000 miles, one of the longest migrations of any known mammal today.

Some populations will hunt cooperatively using a technique called 'bubble netting', whereby individuals gather together as a group and synchronize their movements, creating a circle and blowing bubbles as they go, making the circle smaller. This pushes the fish up to the surface until they have no escape route and then the humpbacks will assemble in the circle to feed through their baleen mouth plates, which engulf the fish and filter the water out. This technique, along with their other traits, is an indication that they are highly intelligent beings, making our persecution of them for hundreds of years even more sobering.

Filled with anticipation for a further 20 minutes, I keep my eyes narrowed and focused out to sea. I cling onto my tripod and camera for dear life as it feels like they could take off at any second. With every wave and swell looking to me like a humpback, I fear that I've started to make things up in my head. I've had this before when filming bears and wolves in Finland up on the Russian boarder in midsummer. My camera operator Benn and I had to stay awake right the way through a night that never got dark, keeping our eyes glued to the edges of the forest for hours on end. By the end of it we started seeing things, thinking the flash of a long-tailed tit was the flicker of a wolf's grey-white fur, and that a glimpse of a red squirrel's tail just had to be a bear cub. Delusion has fully set in as I sit here being thrashed by the elements on the North Cornwall coast.

I give it another 20 minutes and then the conditions start to worsen, as a downpour of pelting rain joins the uncompromising wind. 'That's it,' I say to myself, 'time to go.' I pack my camera back in my bag as my fingers are now bright red and numb with the cold.

Did I see a humpback whale? In all honesty, I can't say. The sighting of whatever it was had been fleeting and, given the conditions, I simply can't confirm what I saw that December day. Given that their numbers are on the increase though, and that sightings are becoming more regular around the Cornwall coast, I haven't given up hope of seeing a humpback whale in my home waters. I still dream of getting a shot of one of the most impressive marine mammals found in our oceans today: the big wings of New England.

# PINKS AND BLUES IN THE WINTER WOODLANDS

I walk along a small muddy path with my pockets full of sunflower hearts. Just to the right of me is a network of small ponds and a bubbling stream. The leafless barren trees seem more alive somehow with the sound of birdsong, as I hear the melancholy call of a blackbird accompanied by some feisty blue tits, robins and a distant nuthatch.

The ponds are busy. Mallard ducks are occupying themselves looking for tasty winter treats, with many congregating around the edges waiting for a passer-by to throw in some bread. Moorhens sneak in and out of the surrounding vegetation, occasionally letting out their resounding call as a pair of mute swans regally glide across the water's surface. I hear a great spotted woodpecker drumming from afar as I look up and see a pair of rooks sitting on the low-hanging branches of a bare tree, their ghoulish beaks prominent, extending to their eyes, and their black glossy plumage, almost blue in parts, making the frigid winter woodlands seem even colder, as grey squirrels scuttle on the ground below.

I pull my woolly black headband further down across my forehead and pull out my gloves. It's cold today, a mere 4°C (39°F).

Carrying on down the path I'm headed to one of my most reliable spots, and the reason my pockets are full of sunflower hearts. There's hardly a time when I have come here and the great tits haven't come to feed out of my hand. This is a well-known spot in Cornwall where the birds have become quite tame and are so used to people that it's as if they almost expect their daily visitors with handfuls of highly calorific snacks, especially in the winter!

Located between Portreath and Godrevy are Tehidy Woods, formally known as Tehidy Country Park. Spread over 250 acres of it is the largest area of woodland in west Cornwall, with over 9 miles of pathways, meadows and lakes. It is an incredibly popular spot for visitors, but it is also amazing for wildlife. Badger setts dominate the interior under the towering broadleaf trees, and roe deer, tawny owls and foxes can all be seen here quite frequently. During the winter months it is one of my favourite places in the area to visit, especially to try to hand-feed the birds.

I turn the corner and sit on one of the old fallen trees close to the scrubby bushes. This is the spot I've always had the best luck with, and I pull out my bag of sunflower hearts pouring a substantial amount into my right hand and extend my arm out towards the nearest bush. 'That should do it,' I say to myself. It's a handful that surely no one could resist!

Within seconds I'm joined by a grey squirrel. Inquisitive yet cautious, it's coming closer towards me, occasionally stopping to stand up on its hind legs to sniff the air and shake its fluffy grey tail. Poor grey squirrels; I do feel sorry for them. It's not their fault they were introduced to the UK in 1876 as an ornamental species for the grand gardens of our stately homes. Of course, they didn't stay as an ornamental species for long and, doing what squirrels do, they escaped and quickly colonized the country, outcompeting our native reds for food and resources. Greys are the carriers of squirrel pox but, being asymptomatic carriers, this deadly virus has no effect on the greys themselves since they evolved with the virus in

North America and built up a lasting immunity to it. But of course this was the first time that red squirrels had come into contact with the virus, and squirrel pox ravaged populations across the UK, wiping out red squirrels from nearly their whole former range and pushing them to the brink of extinction. It's still a huge issue today. The grey squirrel has become demonized here because of the devastating impact on our native reds, but as I look down at this fluffy grey with its long whiskers, I think: it's not their fault. They didn't ask to come to the UK to decorate our gardens; the fault of what's happened to our squirrel population lies with us, and us alone.

I look up and see a flutter in the bushes: a streak of a greenish yellow flank with a prominent white cheek patch and a shimmering black, almost blue, head plumage. It's a great tit!

I stretch my hand out further towards the bushes and I can see him moving from branch to branch, stopping every now and then to take a good look at my cold hand brimming with sunflower hearts. He is clearly thinking about it, but is still slightly wary – so I stay deadly still and don't move a muscle. I have had my arm stretched out now for what must be a good 20 minutes and it starts to shake with its own weight. My other elbow is resting on my knee, and I'm holding my iPhone, all ready with the slow motion function should he come closer. Slowly and cautiously he comes to the nearest thin branch next to my hand, and I press my thumb on the video button to start recording.

In what seems like a millisecond the great tit all of a sudden takes to the air and swoops down onto my icy fingertips. Its tiny claws grasp my skin like tickly little pins – so light you can barely feel them. With his bright and inquisitive eyes he carefully inspects the sunflower hearts in the palm of my hand, initially picking one up in his beak before dropping it back into the pile. He then picks up another and in a flash spreads his wings and heads back into the safety of the bushes.

Having a bird feed out of your hand is a connection with nature like nothing else. It awakens your inner small child. An exchange from one species to another: it is more than magical.

Filled with elation I decide to keep my arm stretched out in the hope that the great tit might come back, as I can still see it flitting around in the undergrowth. But then out of the corner of my eye I see a flash of dusty pink and striking azure blue in the understory, roughly 10m (33ft) from where I'm sitting. This is closely followed by a signature screeching call. With my arm still stretched out cupping the sunflower hearts I twist my body towards the call and let out a tiny gasp. If it is what I think it is, it will be one of my favourite UK birds, and one that is not often seen. During the spring and summer months they will stay quite hidden away in dense woodlands, but during the autumn and winter, if you are lucky, you will see them hopping around on the ground looking for acorns to add to their winter cache. They are our most colourful corvid and, in my opinion, one of our most striking birds.

I stay completely still as the screeching stops and then see a rustling of some leaf litter just behind one of the towering old oaks before, with a skip and a hop, it appears! In all of its glory and magnificent jewel-like plumage, making the cold woodland just that little bit brighter. It's a jay!

Remarkable mimics famous for their ability to imitate the calls of other birds, jays, like all corvids, are known for their intelligence. Vocal mimicry is something that is thought to have evolved in them to help when foraging. They will mimic the calls of predators or other birds to potentially confuse or distract their competitors.

They also have the ability to use tools and can problem-solve, by using twigs or leaves to extract food. They will mislead potential thieves from their winter stashes and will deceive other jays into thinking their cache is in one place, when in fact it is in another. They have good spatial memory, and keep numerous winter stores that they are able to locate when needed. It must be said, however, that many of their acorn supplies do get forgotten about. One study carried out in woodlands of lowland England found that jays were unwittingly responsible for planting more than half of the forest's oak trees, making them one of the most important bird species for the woodland ecosystem and its regeneration in the UK.

I hastily fumble around trying to get the sunflower hearts back into my coat pocket with many of them falling on the ground – much to the delight of the fluffy grey squirrel who bounds over to them now as they scatter around me. I take my bag off my back and pull out my camera. The jay doesn't seem bothered by my presence, enthralled as it is in the ground below, collecting acorns. I swing my camera up and zoom in as far as my lens allows to take some shots, thinking just how beautiful the jay is! There really is no other bird like it in the UK, and each time I see one here it is always like my first!

Suddenly, a family walk round the corner and two small children come screaming down the path, putting the raucous call of any nearby moorhen to shame. The jay swoops off into the canopy, screeching as it goes. They are only toddlers, and are dressed in full-body winter puffer suits. If they didn't look so cute I would be pretty annoyed, but this pair of little teddy bears are far too adorable.

As the family continues down the track into the woodland and out of sight, I look back through my photographs. I've managed to get some really nice close-ups of the face, with its piercing eyes and black cheek patch, the white head plumage and neck, dappled with flecks of black tapering down to that gorgeous dusty pink plumage. And I'm very pleased!

As I go to leave I think – what a morning it's been! Hand-feeding great tits, the rooks and the sound of the nuthatch; the drums of a great spotted woodpecker; a friendly grey squirrel; and, to top it all off, the incredible sightings of a jay. This time of year in Cornwall, if you know where to look, can be one of the most enthralling for wildlife, especially when you are lucky enough to encounter the pinks and blues in the winter woodlands.

# FOREVER A WINTER
# FRIEND

The time is 8am, and the date is 23 December. The sun is just appearing on this cold crisp morning, the horizon painted with hues of indigo, lavender and rose-like orange. Its delicate rays pierce through the frosty air, scattering a golden-white glow across the estuary as a curfew of curlews take flight from the frost-kissed mudflats, their haunting call filling the air. With a wingspan of around 100cm (39½in) they are our largest wading bird in the UK (in fact, the largest in Europe) and are impressive birds. We are lucky to have quite a few here in Newquay and I see and hear them regularly when Isabelle and I come to the Gannel, but, sadly, they are a red-listed species. There are around 58,000 breeding pairs in the summer and it is thought that the UK and Ireland are responsible for around 30 per cent of the world's nesting population, making the ones here of international importance. Our resident birds are then joined during the winter months by curlews migrating to our shores, swelling the total to around 125,000!

There aren't 125,000 curlews down the Gannel estuary this morning – a girl can only dream! But there are at least 25! Still an excellent curfew! (Curfew, or salon or skein, is the name for a group of curlew.)

It's just a few days before Christmas and I still have so much to do. I arrived back in the UK the previous day, having been filming for the best part of a month in the tropics, and Christmas, needless to say, has been the last thing on my mind. I have sent no cards, bought no gifts. I don't even have a tree. This is one of the hardest parts of the job, being away so much: you do miss a lot. Birthdays, get-togethers, births and weddings are all part of being an adult human, but you rarely get to show up to them once you've chosen this lifestyle. As the old saying goes, however, once you find something you love you never have to work another day in your life, and there has never been a truer word spoken. I pinch myself at just how lucky I am to be in this position, and I wouldn't change it for the world. Not one bit of it. My friends and family are used to it now, too, so when we do get together it is even more special.

Isabelle and I continue down the frost-laden path and beside us is a patch of hogweed. Silhouetted against the sun as it creeps across the estuary, the plant's dried seed heads look like lace covered in the morning frost. I take a closer look and it produces a warm rush of serenity – a feast for the eyes! Hogweeds are a perfect example of natural fractals. Observable in the leaves of plants, snowflakes, pine cones, succulents and ferns, to name just a few, these symmetrical geometrical patterns are ubiquitous in nature, and it has been found that just looking at them can significantly reduce our stress levels and mental fatigue. Nature's architecture is good for us.

We turn the corner towards an old rickety washed-up boat that has been here for as long as I can remember. It's surrounded by dense berry-laden hedgerow, an impenetrable mass of bramble, hawthorn, blackthorn and holly. The deep-red holly berries with their evergreen spiky leaves are covered in crystal-like frost. 'Now it feels a bit like Christmas!' I say to Isabelle, her silly smiling face staring up at me with sheer love. She has missed her mummy while

I've been away, and hasn't left my side since I returned – she never does. A true mummy's girl through and through.

Before I head out for the rest of the day to do my last-minute Christmas shopping I have come to this corner to see if I can meet someone, someone I have been seeing here the few months. And this corner of the hedgerow is most certainly its patch. My coat pocket still has an ample supply of sunflower hearts in it so I can be ready at any opportunity.

I sit down on the wood of the old icy boat and then I hear its call, the cheery and melodic trills carrying through the crisp frosty air, warming my heart with every chirp. I look around to see where it is, and lo and behold, perched on the blackthorn next to me, I see its plump orange-red breast with white underneath, the sandy-brown back almost silver grey in parts, and its tiny glistening eyes. My friend has come to see me! The robin!

Synonymous with winter and on pretty much every Christmas card, the robin is officially the nation's favourite bird. Their charming yet feisty demeanour and their singing right the way through the dark, cold, winter months have made them a species that captivates hearts. Known to be highly territorial, robins sing throughout the year and during the winter to defend or establish their territories, and their singing helps them to maintain ownership over their favoured area. They are also known to start breeding quite early in the year, often in January, so singing during the hardest of months not only advertises their presence to potential mates, but also shows off their fitness. Their songs are a way of communicating with one another as well as warning off potential threats. While it may be very enjoyable for us to hear them during winter, singing expends a lot of energy, and the reasons for it are complex and multifaceted.

The robin's history with humans goes back centuries and they have been written about for many years. Their delightful habit of following us around, particularly in gardens, has made us adore them even more. But they do this for very good reason as they associate us with food. Every time a gardener turns the soil they uncover a buffet of tasty worms and invertebrates for robins to eat. It has even been suggested that they think we are large wild pigs, as this is the same behaviour they display when pigs are turning the ground. I can't possibly comment on what robins think about us, but their cultural significance and our association with them throughout history are clear.

The robin looks down at me, then jumps a little further onto some of the closest branches while singing its trilling tune ever so softly. It is now so close that if I stretched out my hand I could touch it. I rummage around in my pocket for some sunflower hearts and place my hand on the old wood on the front side of the boat, as close to the robin as possible. I've been working on this hand-feeding thing over the last few months whenever Isabelle and I have come for a walk to the Gannel. The first few times the robin flew away, then it started to come a bit closer, until one day it stood on my hand – twice! Both times it was collecting sunflower hearts to eat. But it has been quite a while since I was last here, having been away, and I hope it remembers me.

It flies down onto the icy boat, directly to the left of my fingers, and looks me in the eye. I like to think that this is the robin saying hello, but of course I will never know. Then, with the lightness of a feather, it jumps onto my hand and starts to feed, looking up in between each sunflower seed directly at me! 'Hello, lovely one,' I whisper under my breath as the robin seems to reply with a soft trill. It stays on my hand for a good two minutes, which is substantial progress from when we first met a few months ago! And I am in my element!

Then it lets out a few chirps and flies back off into the hedgerow, quite far away this time, and I get the sense that it has had its fill. The time is now 10.30am. The sun has risen and the estuary has woken up. The crystal-like frost is almost thawing before my eyes, and the leaves that were icy masterpieces just a few short hours ago are covered in tiny gem-like droplets of water. I hear the shouts of dog walkers and families that have descended to the estuary for their pre-Christmas walks. 'Should we go?' I say, turning to Isabelle, and she wags her tail as if to say 'yes, Mummy'.

As we walk back up the hill and into town I finally feel Christmassy. I'm excited for the festivities that the next few days will bring: mulled wine by the bucketload, twinkling lights, mince pies and brandy butter following a delicious nut roast with roast potatoes. Sitting with my oldest friends talking absolute nonsense for hours and opening my ridiculously odd presents from my mother – a long-standing Christmas tradition in our house.

And it's all thanks to the robin down the estuary. I hadn't felt like it was Christmas at all until he came to say hello. Nature and wildlife do powerful things to us, whether we realize it or not.

Spending time with wild species is nothing short of magnificent, and when they become relaxed in our presence, it is something even more magical. Not all species will feed out of your hand like the friendly robin, and many absolutely shouldn't, and we should not want them to or try to habituate them. Each species has its role and its place, and we should respect each animal for what they are and for their vital role in each ecosystem. Every animal on Earth feels just like we do: they have families, emotions and complex relationships, and are masters of their own environments. We are just a small part of all life, and we need to respect every other living creature as we would want to be respected ourselves. The human race cannot survive without nature and without every living organism that makes up our wondrous planet, which is why every single thing must be protected for the future, however big or small.

From the foxes and dolphins to the badger cubs and tawny owlets. From polecats in the dead of night to our colourful choughs, kingfishers and the parrots of the sea. From our migrating cuckoos, swallows, osprey and short-eared owls to the fairies dancing in the dunes. From the great crested grebe and buzzards, to the mice that live among us. The biodiversity that we have here in Cornwall is nothing short of extraordinary, and we are incredibly lucky to be able to share this marvellous county with equally magnificent wildlife. This is why it is up to all of us to look after it – every single species and every single individual.

And this includes my friendly robin, forever a winter friend.

# FURTHER RESOURCES

British Divers Marine Life Rescue
bdmlr.org.uk

British Trust for Ornithology's cuckoo tracking project
www.bto.org/cuckoos

Cornish Seal Sanctuary
sealsanctuary.sealifetrust.org/en

Cornwall Beaver Project
www.cornwallwildlifetrust.org.uk/what-we-do/our-conservation-work/
on-land/cornwall-beaver-project

Cornwall Bird Watching and Preservation Society (CBWPS)
cbwps.org.uk

Cornwall Mammal Group
www.cornwallmammalgroup.org

Cornwall Seal Group Research Trust
www.cornwallsealgroup.co.uk

Cornwall Wildlife Trust
www.cornwallwildlifetrust.org.uk

Padstow Sealife Safaris
www.padstowsealifesafaris.co.uk

Prickles & Paws Hedgehog Rescue
www.pricklesandpaws.org

Royal Society for the Protection of Birds (RSPB)
www.rspb.org.uk

# ACKNOWLEDGEMENTS

Writing this book in the hardest year of my adult life has been no easy feat. I would like to thank some people here for their support throughout this process and through everything this year has thrown at me. Without them, this book – alongside pretty much everything else – simply wouldn't have happened. A few words on the back pages of a nature book cannot do these people justice for how they have supported and helped me this year, but one day I only hope I'm able to help them should they ever need it.

Mum: thank you for the silliness, the latest badger news and garden updates, the hand-knitted jumpers that could fit a small village in them, the eclectic dinners and everything else in between. I have never met another human quite like you, and I wouldn't have it any other way.

Dad: thank you for always being there for me, even though you live a million miles away. I always know you are there when things get tough and I miss you every day.

Dave: my mate Dr Dave Hudson, thank you for being one of my best friends, my on-hand councillor, my advisor, my housemate, my business partner and basically my brother. Nothing would have happened this year without you – you're the kindest most generous man I know.

Jessie Stewart and Natel Mounsey: thank you to my oldest friends for always being there for me throughout everything and rallying in an instant when I've needed it. I'm eternally, forever grateful to you and am incredibly lucky to have you in my life. Also, to Ruth Luck, Chloe Lyme, Kirsty Dickens and Kayleigh Rees – my loves forever.

Thank you to my management, Grainne Montgomery, Sarah Moorhouse and Kate Landy: you make my life infinitely better every single day! Your unwavering support and constant belief in me make me realize that anything is possible, and I can't thank you enough.

To Alison Hitchens: thank you for FaceTiming me every single day in my darkest time to make sure I was OK. You are one of the best humans I know and I can't imagine my life without you.

To Ruth Levis: you have had my back since day one of this crazy ride and have supported me through everything! You are my queen and I love you with every bit of me.

Thank you to Emily Bates for being a wonderful human and constantly supporting me this year. To Sean Ryan for the constant laughs and your hilarious and impeccable editing, and to Philip Edwards for your support and the impromptu hotel room dancing.

To Megan McCubbin: thank you for being one of my best friends and always being there for me. I'm forever grateful to you for everything and for your continued support every single day.

To Sophie Pavelle, my wizard unicorn bear: thank you for your words of wisdom throughout and always being there for me. Let's adventure soon.

Thank you to my other great friends Ben Morrison, Elie Gordon, Hannah Spencer-Hall and Stacey Skelly: even though we are unable to see each other as much now, I know you are always there.

To Adam Pearce: thank you for making me whole again and everything else in between, we have all of the adventures to come!

And thank you to Lucy Lapwing, Leif Bersweden, James Stevens and Jack Baddams for the constant laughs, daftness and ridiculousness: I wouldn't be without you.